DECONSTRUCTING THE LEFT:

From Vietnam to the Persian Gulf

by

Peter Collier
and
David Horowitz

D0062974

A *Second Thoughts* Book

Published by
Second Thoughts Books and
Center for the Study of Popular Culture

4720 Boston Way
Lanham, Maryland 20706

3 Henrietta Street
London WC2E 8LU England

Distributed by National Book Network

The paper used in this publication meets the minimum
requirements of American National Standard for
Information Sciences—Permanence of Paper for
Printed Library Materials, ANSI Z39.48–1984.♾™
Manufactured in the United States of America.

Library of Congress Cataloging-in-Publication Data
Collier, Peter.
Deconstructing the Left : from Vietnam to the Persian Gulf
/ by Peter Collier and David Horowitz.
p.   cm.
1. United States—Social conditions—1960-1980.
2. United States—Social conditions—1980-
3. Right and left (Political science)
4. Radicalism—United States—History—20th century.
I. Horowitz, David.   II. Title.
HN59.C62   1991   306'.0973—dc20   91-23478 CIP

ISBN 0-8191-8315-6 (pbk., alk. paper)

British Cataloging in Publication Information Available

CONTENTS

The Great White Whale

If the end of the Cold War marks a triumph for America, it also marks a paradox. All over the world, people who cherish and seek freedom look to this country and its political ideals for inspiration and support. For rebels in Afghanistan and Kurdish refugees in Iraq, for Chinese protesters in Tienanmen Square and for East Berliners tearing down the Wall of their bondage, the United States is indeed — and has been during the entire postwar period — the leader of the free world, and the light at the end of their tunnel. For the oppressed of the world, therefore, the political culture of America is the culture of freedom.

But here, at home, in the very institutions of that culture, there is a different feeling. The self-doubt that paralyzed Americans after the Vietnam War may have been purged in part by the recent triumph in the Gulf, but its half-life still lingers, cherished by political Leftists for whom America will always be the enemy rather than the liberator. Entrenched, as never before, on the faculties of our elite universities, these Leftists try to indoctrinate the next generation of Americans in the discredited ideologies of the radical past, portraying this country as a predatory and imperialist power, a wellspring of racism and sexism and of the oppressive culture of dead white European males.

Among academic intellectuals, the leading philosophical doctrines — Marxism(!), structuralism, deconstructionism, etc. — are rooted in intellectual and political traditions that gave rise to Nazism and Communism, the twin scourges of the 20th Century. The thrust of these doctrines is to question and deconstruct democratic traditions and values, to instill a sense of moral relativism and moral equivalency, and to question objectivity and truth itself. In this atmosphere of distortion and propaganda, America's tolerance and freedom are indistinguishable from totalitarian force. It is hardly an accident that the university based intelligentsia has been the center of relentless attacks on America's national security apparatus and its policies for the last 25 years, or that it has been the focus of opposition to America's recent effort to lead a multinational coalition against Iraq's aggression in the Persian Gulf.

We were once a part of this Left, having edited the radical magazine *Ramparts*, in the late Sixties and early Seventies. Our Leftism ended with the end of the Vietnam War, which revealed to us the real consequences of America's defeat for the people of Indochina and the rest of the world. We saw how the Left which claimed to care about the fate of the Cambodians and the Vietnamese while the war was raging, really didn't care at all once the United States had lost and their oppressors were Communists. What the Left really cared about was that America should be defeated.

This experience began our "second thoughts," and with them a renewed engagement with American radicalism. But we weren't marching anymore. Rather than being engaged *for* the Left, we were engaged against it. In a feature article in the Washington *Post* (reprinted here as "Goodbye to All That"), we explained how, in the 1984 elections, we had come to vote for the man we had loved to hate in the Sixties, Ronald Reagan. What we were really writing about, however, was our disgust with the hypocritical and self-dramatizing anti-Americanism that had become the core belief of American Leftists, and how we ourselves had come to appreciate the human rights and blessings of the country we had been born to, which we and our comrades, in the Sixties, had set out to destroy.

Following the *Post* article, we found ourselves at the barricades again, but this time facing the Left rather than shoulder to shoulder with it. This book is a record of these skirmishes. It should be read with the understanding that the pieces which comprise it were written in the heat of political battle. Some were originally given as speeches at the colleges our old comrades have done so much to politicize and whose intellectual atmosphere they have so cynically debased ("May Day 1990" and "Angela Davis and Me"). Some were articles that appeared in various magazines, often for polemical occasions. "A Decade Overrated and Unmourned," for instance, was our side of a print debate over retrospective assessments of the Sixties. "Racial Consciousness" and "The New Racism and the Radical Left" attempted to hold radicals to account for betraying the civil rights ideals with which the Sixties had started."Keepers of the Flame" was a reply to Leftist critics of our book *Destructive Generation* who tried to pin the sins of the decade on *us* — and thus absolve themselves from any responsibility for the disasters they had collectively helped to create. This was the perfect analog to Leftists' disavowal, shortly afterwards, of responsibility for the catastrophes of "actually existing socialism" in the Soviet bloc. In effect they were copping Bart Simpson's plea: "I didn't do it. You didn't see me do it. You can't pin that on me." Other pieces were engagements with the emerging movements of the "Next Left", which had risen from the ashes of the movement we had abandoned ("The Sixties and the Eighties," "From Red to Green," "The 'Peace' Movement" and "The War They Lost").

One of our friends once said that lapsed radicals like ourselves are always condemned to regard the Left as their Great White Whale. There is probably an element of truth in this. If so, this book is a record of our sightings of the beast. We may not yet have set the final harpoon, but we have given chase. □

I

The Sixties:
Acts and Aftermaths

Chapter One

A Decade Overrated and Unmourned

(Peter Collier & David Horowitz)

From its earliest battle cry — "You can't trust anyone over 30" — until the end of its brief strut on the stage of national attention, the Sixties generation saw itself as a scouting party for a new world. It was the master of ceremonies presenting a "cultural revolution" that would better the lot of inmates in the prison of linear thought. It was the social horticulturist whose "greening of America" would allow the long stalled post-industrialist age finally to break through the crust of the Puritan past. It was the avenging angel that would destroy the evil empire of "Amerika" and free the captive peoples of color around the world. The Sixties generation had created a new age, the Age of Aquarius, whose kingdom was surely at hand.

It is little wonder that people who lived through the Sixties, or who felt the nostalgia for it that such films as *The Big Chill* conveyed, regard this decade as the last good time. The images that remain are of youth — kids arriving in buses from all over America to converge on Haight-Ashbury, kids sharing their dope and bodies with newcomers who dropped into their communes, kids with pictures of outlaw heroes such as Bonnie and Clyde on their walls. It was a time of eternal youth: even the adults acted like kids.

Has any other generation ever been so successful in promoting its claims of Utopia? Looking at the era two decades later, we only see the images which reflected in the glass of Sixties narcissism. We are assured that it was a time of great idealism populated by individuals who wanted nothing more than to give peace a chance; a time when dewy-eyed young people in the throes of moral passion sought only to remake the world. Were they driven to extreme remedies? It was because that world

---

A version of this chapter originally appeared in Playboy, *January 1989.*

was governed by cruel power. Did they burn out quickly? It was because a dark world needed their glorious light.

The reality, of course, was less exalted. If not quite the low dishonest decade of the Thirties, the Sixties was nonetheless a time when what began as American mischief matured into real destructiveness. It was a time when a gang of ghetto thugs like the Black Panthers could be anointed as political visionaries; when Merry Pranksters of all stripes went into business as social evangelists spreading a chemical gospel. It was the most self-dramatizing of decades, a time when the only indispensable props were a soapbox, a megaphone and a suppository.

If God had died in the Fifties, the victim in the Sixties was the "System," that collection of inherited values and assumptions which provide guidelines for the individual and the nation. As one center of authority after another was discredited under our assault, we convinced ourselves that we murdered to create. But what we proposed to put in the place of destroyed authority — a new social order, a new system of human relationships — turned out to be dangerous Utopias infected with banal dreams and totalitarian passions.

*   *   *

New decades rarely start on time. The election of John Kennedy, however, was such a calculated attempt to break with the past, substituting youth for Eisenhower's age and "vigor" for the old President's evident exhaustion with the ambiguities of the post-war world, that 1960 seemed like a watershed moment. Kennedy did lend the office an existential *brio*, but his thousand days were spent playing out the themes of the Fifties. What we think of as the Sixties — that historical interlude that would have such a distinctive style and tone — really began the day the assassin came to Dallas. The "lone crazed gunman," a specter that would haunt the era, had been loosed. JFK became a melancholy ghost rattling his chains for the rest of the decade — a symbol first of its betrayed promise and eventually of its corrupted innocence.

Even during his three years in office Kennedy had been a bystander of the most crucial event of the beginning of the decade. This was the civil rights movement, which opened America to its black outcasts. The summary moment of the civil rights movement came three months before Kennedy's death when Martin Luther King stood in front of the Lincoln Memorial and delivered his "I Have A Dream" speech. It seemed at the time that the speech might have set the tone for the Sixties. What was surprising about King's movement, however, was not how quickly it arrived (it was preeminently a movement of the Fifties), but how quickly it passed.

By 1965, when the "high" Sixties was in gear, King was on the defensive, under attack by a new radical generation. With Stokely Carmichael as their representative figure, black militants rejected non-violence and social integration, calling instead for "black power." They used threats of violence to exclude traditional civil rights leaders like Roy Wilkins and Whitney Young from their protest and put pressure on King himself. The torching of the urban ghettos, beginning with Watts in 1965, provided the light by which the black power movement wrote a violent and chaotic epilogue to King's history of decency and courage.

King continued to speak, before diminishing audiences, about peaceful and creative change, about building a movement of love and hope. The black activists opposed to him rode his coattails at the same time they were privately deriding him as "Uncle Martin" and "de Lawd." In a gesture characteristic of the nihilism which was coming to be the most typical feature of Sixties politics, they made it clear that they wanted no part of King's American dream. They were not interested in being integrated into a System they had decided was irredeemably racist; in fact they wanted only to bring the System to its knees. King talked about brotherhood; Carmichael preached the doctrine that blacks were a "colony" and called for "national liberation" from America itself.

The guerrilla army of this liberation was to be the Black Panthers. While King had enriched the national dialogue on race and civil rights, the Panthers completed the debasement of political language and process with totalitarian slogans such as "off the pigs" and "Power grows out of the barrel of a gun," and "If you're not part of the solution you're part of the problem." As investigations revealed later on, they were using the Santa Cruz mountains as a killing fields to solve their internal struggles for power at the same time they were using rhetoric to titillate whites momentarily enamored of "revolutionary violence."

Except for the Panthers' murders of a few of their own and their gun battles with local police, black militancy was primarily talk. But even talk had consequences. A daunting example of the impact that the loose talk and heavy rhetoric of the Sixties had on policy can be seen in the way the black family — a time bomb ticking with growing ominousness then and exploding with daily detonations today — got pushed off the political agenda.

While Carmichael, Huey Newton and others were launching a revolutionary front against the system, the Johnson administration was contemplating a commitment to use the power of the federal government to end the economic and social inequalities that still plagued American blacks. A Presidential task force under Daniel Patrick Moynihan was given the mandate to identify the obstacles preventing blacks from seizing opportunities that had been grasped by other minority groups in the previous fifty years of American history. About the same time as the passage of the Voting Rights Act of 1965, Moynihan published findings which emphasized the central importance of family in shaping an individual life and noted with alarm that 21 percent of black families were headed by single women. "[The] one unmistakable lesson in American history," he warned, is that a country that allows "a large number of young men to grow up in broken families, dominated by women, never acquiring any stable relationship to male authority, never acquiring any set of rational expectations about the future — that community asks for and gets chaos. Crime, violence, unrest, disorder — most particularly the furious, unrestrained lashing out at the whole social structure — that is not only to be expected; it is very near to inevitable."

Moynihan proposed that the government confront this problem as a priority, but his conclusions were bitterly attacked by the black radicals and white liberals, joined in an alliance of anger and self-flagellation, which soon closed the window of opportunity Moynihan had opened by condemning his report as racist not only in its conclusions but also in its conception. (It had failed to stress the evils of the "capitalistic system.") This rejectionist coalition did not want a program for social change so much as a confession of guilt. For them the only "non-racist" gesture the President could make would be acceptance of their demand for $400 million in "reparations" for 400 years of slavery. The White

House retreated before this onslaught and took the black family off the agenda. As Moynihan said later, "From being buoyantly open to ideas and enterprises, [Johnson] became near contemptuous of civil rights leaders who he now believed cared only for symbols." In his next State of the Union address, the President devoted only 45 words of his speech to the problems confronting blacks.

It is an archetypal Sixties case history — the rejection of real solutions in favor of demands which are made with the knowledge that they cannot be met. The consequences of this syndrome have become, with time, painfully clear. While in 1950 some 30% of Americans had been poor (according to the official definition of poverty), the normal workings of the system had reduced this figure to 13% by 1968 when Great Society programs were just beginning. Over the next twelve years federal spending on poverty would quadruple. But without the intended effect: in 1980, 13% of Americans were still classified as poor, the same figure as 12 years and more than $100 billion earlier. What *had* changed was the nature of poverty itself. It had become increasingly youthful, black, feminized, and entrenched. Unwed black teen mothers had become the norm rather than the exception in the black community.

It is a problem that the present day apologists for the Sixties blame on the System too. By as early as 1970, however, black families that were intact and living outside the South, in which both adults had a high school education, had attained income equality with their white counterparts. These were blacks who had remained committed to the opportunity system Martin Luther King had embraced. These are the blacks who today have entered the professional and managerial class in huge numbers, an increase of 63% during the Eighties alone, a decade when, for the first time in U.S. history, the black middle class outnumbered the poor.

But radical leaders who had pushed King aside continued to condemn the System and advised blacks to buy out of it so vehemently that a commitment to self-betterment almost had to be made against the grain of black life. In 1950, when America *did* have a racist system but did not have a self-anointed priesthood preaching about its evils, 9.5% of black teenagers (as opposed to (8.7% of whites) were unemployed. In 1980, after a decade and a half of Sixties rhetoric, some 38% of black teenagers were unemployed. Obviously the bad-mouthing of America was not the only cause for this disastrous turn of events, but it was an instance of contributory negligence on the part of radicals. A part of the black community has made advances since 1960. But their accomplishments are *in spite* of Sixties figures like Stokely Carmichael, who opted for a privileged exile in totalitarian Guinea after a frightening run-in with the Panthers, or like Huey Newton, who was charged with one felony after another before his sordid death on an Oakland street corner in 1989. The success of the black middle class is a reward for following Martin Luther King's advice to commit itself to the American dream, while others were remaining trapped in the self-pitying victimhood so adroitly exploited by radical demagogues.

Black radicals who reviled King during his lifetime as an Uncle Tom now kneel with cynical reverence at his shrine, although they still reject his vision. Blacks still face poverty and unemployment, but chief among their disabilities are Sixties leftovers like the opportunistic Jesse Jackson who have revived the anti-Americanism and infatuation with Third World totalitarianism exhibited by King's radical opponents twenty years ago. How would King have regarded Jackson's remarks about "Hymies" and his praise for a black fascist like Louis Farrakhan? Probably in much the same way he regarded white demagogues in the Sixties who talked about "niggers" and praised white fascists in robes.

*   *   *

Another reason for the degradation of the Civil Rights movement was the willingness of its radical leaders to buy into the notion, part of the vulgar Marxism in vogue during the Sixties, that blacks were victims not only of discrimination and prejudice but of the American empire itself, of *Amerika*. Like other destructive ideas that fastened themselves like an exotic jungle fungus on our national self-conception, this notion came directly by way of Vietnam.

If civil rights was the central movement of the Sixties, Vietnam was the central fact. It informed the life of an entire generation. The war was such a pervasive experience that even non-combatants felt as though they had been waist-deep in rice paddies and occasionally experienced a sudden stab of fear at the staccato rhythms of helicopter blades. The war continues to be fought well into the Eighties in literature and film as well as in foreign policy. Should the U.S. have gone into Vietnam? Could we have won?

To argue these questions is to become mired in the battles long after the war is lost. It is also to lose sight of the most important fact about Vietnam: it was a cultural occasion as much as an historical event. The destructive anti-Americanism that eventually came to characterize the era had been off limits, intellectually and morally at the beginning of the decade; the Vietnam war was the justification the Movement needed to cross the line.

The first anti-war protests — by those who had been part of the civil rights movement as it developed under King — were caused by what was perceived as the inhumanity of the war. But this moral dimension was soon replaced in the anti-war movement by an irrational hatred of America and all it stood for. (The war corrupted everything — the people who protested against it as well as those who fought.) The Movement soon determined that what it perceived as the lies of the U.S. government must be fought by lies of its own. These lies ranged from the sentimental (Ho Chi Minh — a lifelong Comintern agent — was simply a misunderstood nationalist, the George Washington of his country) to the strategic (North Vietnamese regular troops were not fighting in the South alongside the NLF). Truth was the first casualty — in the war at home as much as the one in Vietnam.

After it was over and Movement "activists" (as the media generously called them) were looking for a way to make their revolt seem like a patriotic act, they created the myth that they had detoured into hardline positions because this was the only way to stop the war. In fact, Vietnam, like Voltaire's God, would have had to be created if it didn't exist because it justified the anti-Americanism that was part of the Movement from its very beginnings. Tom Hayden let that particular cat out of the bag later on, when speaking about the 1962 Port Huron Statement (the founding charter of the Students for a Democratic Society): "We were opposed... to doctrines imposed from the past. In that sense we were not Marxist... But we were conscious of what we were driving at, which was a revolutionary change in the American structure. We were never reformers who became disillusioned and, therefore, more radical." In other words the war in Vietnam was a gift of chance which allowed radical leaders to convince others of the need for a social apocalypse and of the necessity for their destructive strategies.

As the war escalated, the treason of the heart committed by the many became a treason of fact for the few. In 1969, SDS splintered into factions, the chief of which was the Weathermen. That year, its leadership went to Havana to form the Venceremos Brigade. While they were there, they held discussions with the Vietnamese and Cubans which led them to return home committed to a wave of terrorism which was cut short only because their high command blew itself up in a Manhattan townhouse.

Like other wounds suffered by Sixties radicals, this one was self-inflicted. Despite their incessant complaints of police brutality, Sixties radicals lived for the most part in a no-fault system, demanding their Constitutional rights at the same time they were abusing and denouncing the Constitution. They knew they had the option, which many of them ultimately used, of diving back into the "system" when they tired of being extrinsic. (For this reason New Leftism, although discredited in politics, continues to thrive in the "academic work" of former radicals who returned for postgraduate degrees to the universities they had earlier tried to destroy.) It was an example of the cynicism which marked the decade — counting on the fact that America was exactly the sort of flexible and forgiving society they were condemning it for failing to be.

The radicals' assault in the Sixties was never directed against conservatives. The target was liberalism itself. It had been liberalism that had guided America to power in the post-war world. It was liberalism that got the U.S. into Vietnam. It was centrist liberalism which was the balance wheel that gave synchronicity to the entire political system. But now radicals assaulted the center: if it could not hold, then America would fall. Liberals were bashed not only over foreign affairs but also for the domestic program architected by the New Deal. Radicals in the university initiated a systematic revisionism that challenged the whole achievement of the American liberal tradition — from the origins of the Constitution to the origins of the Cold War.

The decisive moment in the assault against liberalism was the destruction of the last Democratic Party presidential candidate in this tradition, Hubert Humphrey. The instrument was the riot, which a handful of radical leaders organized for the 1968 Democratic Party convention in Chicago. Tom Hayden and the other leaders knew that Chicago's mayor Richard Daley, in the wake of the riots after Martin Luther King's assassination, had called for the shooting of "looters" on sight. They knew that "the whole world was watching." They knew that a confrontation in the streets of Chicago would inevitably lead to violence that would explode in political shocks felt across the globe.

The Chicago demonstrations became the Tet Offensive of the anti-war movement: the military defeat on the battlefield that won a political victory in Washington. In the wake of the riots, Humphrey was defeated and four years later the New Left vision possessed the Democratic Party, the "cold war" liberals' ability to fight the takeover having been destroyed by the Chicago debacle. The Left's candidate lost, but its vision prevailed. George McGovern became for the Left what Barry Goldwater had been for the Right eight years earlier — a way of entering and eventually possessing a party. A sign of the times was the way that Tom Hayden, who had destroyed the Democrats' chances in Chicago in 1968, resurfaced as a Party regular in California in the mid-Seventies.

Vietnam was a powerful narcotic. (One of the self-revealing comments of the anti-war movement came when the Communists first agreed to negotiate. "We fight, fight, fight, and then they sell us out!" was the despairing response of Harlem Maoist, Bill Epton.) The Movement was addicted to the sense of being invincibly correct and utterly moral which the war gave it. Thus the feeling of emptiness that came over the Sixties generation when the withdrawal from Vietnam began.

By the time the last U.S. personnel had ingloriously left, Sixties radicals were already searching for new connections (in Africa and Central America) that would restore the high they had lost. They turned their backs on Vietnam. Their moral outrage did not come into play when Hanoi conquered the South. The only "lessons" of Vietnam they were interested in were those that confirmed American guilt. The Left wasn't interested in the curriculum involving Communist genocide in Cambodia or the imperialism of Moscow and Hanoi. Their moral amnesia allowed them to ignore the fact that more Indochinese were killed in the first two years of the Communist peace than had been killed on all sides in a decade of the anti-Communist war.

At the same time that they ignored these realities, the Sixties radicals were making sure that the war, or at least their version of it, would linger in the nation's consciousness. Just as the Sixties had been dominated by the *fact* of Vietnam, so the postwar era was dominated by the Vietnam metaphor. Until the Sixties, the dominant political image had been provided by Munich, which encapsulated the lessons of the Thirties as a warning to democracies to arm themselves against aggressors who talked about peace. But the Munich metaphor was repeatedly assaulted in the Sixties by those who claimed that it had lured us into the Southeast Asian war. In the Seventies, "Munich" was replaced by "Vietnam," an experience with the opposite moral — that anti-communism led to "quagmire" and a vigilant democracy to "abuses of power," and that totalitarian Third World movements were actually manifestations of harmless nationalism.

The Vietnam metaphor dominated the politics of the Eighties as the Vietnam War did the politics of the Sixties. It *made* policy. Whenever America even considered acting in its self-defense, opponents of such action merely invoked the specter of Vietnam. They talked about the "holocaust" in Indochina with full awareness that the symbolic resonance of such a term makes the U.S. comparable to the Nazis. "Another Vietnam" was a curse on action. Less an argument than an incantation, it became an irresistible pressure for passivity, isolationism, and appeasement.

The battle cry "No Vietnams in Central America" showed the Vietnam metaphor in action. The slogan smothered all distinctions of time and place that separated these conflicts and defined their individual meanings. Playing on fears of another quagmire that would again bleed this country, this slogan became a persuasion to do nothing about the expansionism of Marxist-Leninist regimes or about dominoes which might fall in our own hemisphere in a way that they did not in Southeast Asia. For nostalgic radicals, however, "No Vietnams in Central America" was also an unfulfilled wish. The Sixties is still seen as the last good time by these people, who are like the Japanese soldiers wandering in a cerebral jungle unwilling to admit that the war is over. They really *want* another Vietnam — another cultural upheaval; another defeat for the U.S.; another drama of moral self-inflation; another orgy of guilt and recrimination; a reprise, in short, of the Sixties.

In the Vietnam metaphor, we have the tunnel at the end of the light.

* * *

During the Sixties, finally, we became a culture of splinter groups, people who identified ourselves according to ethnicity, gender, special interests — a galaxy of minorities, united only by a sensibility that now regarded society at large with suspicion. The political philosopher Michael Walzer unconsciously expressed this sensibility when he confessed, in a recent article in *The New Republic*, "It is still true that only when I go to Washington to demonstrate do I feel at home there." Within the culture the Sixties created, its minorities exist in perpetual adversarial relationship to America, inspired by assumptions about its malign intent, which they "learned" as a result of the symbiosis between the black revolution and the war in Vietnam. This factionalization and division, this readiness to believe the worst about our homeground, is the enduring legacy of the Sixties.

"Liberation" was the radical watchword. Where did it lead us? No cause followed so swiftly or so instructively along the path cleared by its radical vanguard as that in behalf of American women. Even before feminism was able to proclaim itself as an independent cause of the era, a contrite American power structure had included women in the compact it had made with the civil rights movement led by Martin Luther King. In 1963, the first federal statute requiring "equal pay for equal work" sailed through Congress, and the Civil Rights Act of 1964 specifically extended its protection to women, banning discrimination on the basis of "race, color, religion, sex, or national origin."

But like its black counterpart, the women's movement had already been seized by the radical passion. Its manifesto, Betty Friedan's *The Feminine Mystique*, went beyond a plea for equality in the System to an indictment of the System itself: "Our culture does not permit women to accept or gratify their basic need to grow and fulfill their potentialities as human beings." There was an important truth in the claim that America's women had been denied their place in its dream, a truth that the victories of the next decade would confirm, permanently expanding their horizons and opportunities as dramatically as the civil rights revolution had those of American blacks. But the exaggerations of the indictment were equally important and consequential. The culture that Friedan had indicted because it did not permit women to grow had provided Friedan herself with an Ivy League education, and an opportunity not only to have three children but a writing career subsidized by her working husband. The family which she claimed was a "concentration camp" for American women had supported her in the years of her labor. Far from denying her recognition, her "masculine" profession had rewarded her with the hyperbolic acclaim of reviewers who hailed her work as "the most important book of the 20th century."

But in 1966 when Friedan and her associates founded the National Organization of Women, the radical enthusiasms of the time blinded them to positive American realities like this and committed them instead to a rhetoric that was rejectionist. To the feminists of NOW, women were an "oppressed majority," the victims of a "sexism" which paralleled racism and which was imposed by the "patriarchal" character of the American system. Women's liberation could not be achieved by extending the "rights" of such an oppressive system to American women, but only by a "cultural revolution" that would "restructure" American society, abolishing the "gender roles" that the system had imposed, and legal and moral restraints which denied women control over their bodies and delivered them to "the tyranny of their reproductive biology."

In the name of liberation, the radicals crusaded against laws that recognized differences between men and women and that had provided special protections for women in the workplace, the family and society at large. To the radicals the family was nothing more than a target of opportunity. Gloria Steinem denounced marriage as a form of prostitution, while 50,000 feminists marked the anniversary of women's suffrage with a march on Fifth Avenue and expressive slogans like "Don't Cook Dinner — Starve a Rat Today." Radical feminists linked all the Sixties revolutions: "we want to destroy the three pillars of class and caste society — the family, private property and the state."

Eventually, the sorcerer's apprentices of the feminist movement would draw back in horror from what they had unloosed. Referring to the excessive "Second Wave" of the movement she had begun, Friedan decried the way that the feminine mystique had been superseded "by a *feminist* mystique which denied that core of women's personhood that is fulfilled through love, nurture, home." Feminists like Andrea Dworkin began to warn that "sexual liberation only made life harder for women."

The toll on the emotional life and psyche of a generation from the sexual confusion is difficult to assess. But consequences of the revolutionary feminism that outlasted the Sixties are measurable. Between 1960 and 1980 the percentage of illegitimate births more than doubled. ("Only a minority of American children may now expect to reach age 18 having lived continuously with their natural parents," summarized New York Senator Daniel Moynihan in January 1987. "Sixty percent of children now being born may expect at one time or another to live in a single-parent family and 9 in 10 of such families are headed by females.") Of the nation's 33.7 million poor in 1984, 35% lived in female-headed households. Without the sharp increase in the number of such families, U.S. poverty would have dropped significantly between 1960 and 1984.

Friedan and other feminists may now be chastened by the unforseen consequences of their attack on the American family, but the nation whose institutions they assaulted is finding its equilibrium less easy to recover. As previous revolutions have shown, it is far more difficult to restore protective traditions that have been destroyed than it was to destroy them in the first place.

* * *

This grim historical lesson is underscored by another of the Sixties' cultural liberations, one of the unintended consequences of which is a venereal epidemic that now threatens a death toll many times greater than that of the war in Vietnam. Basking in the reflected glow of the Sixties, gays cast off the chains of a moral tradition they denounced as serving only to "oppress" them and established their own liberated zones where they pursued an ideal of liberated sex for more than a decade. Their bathhouses became institutional symbols and political organizing halls, as well as the sexual gymnasiums of the gay movement. In time, they also came to resemble petri dishes culturing the dangerous diseases that began to afflict the gay community.

Public health officials in San Francisco, Los Angeles and New York watched with alarm as a succession of serious venereal epidemics — rectal gonorrhea, Hepatitis B, CMV — swept through these communities, epidemics so extensive that they cost taxpayers in excess of $1 million a day to provide treatment. In the past, action would have been taken; this time there was no action. The liberated gay culture was *doing its thing*. Public health officials were intimidated from speaking out lest they trespass against a "minority lifestyle;" proven public health measures were rejected as an infringement on "civil rights."[8]

Even after AIDS appeared at the beginning of the Eighties, the situation did not change. In San Francisco, gay activists and their liberal allies in the political machine that controls the city prevented action to close the bathhouses. This coalition obscured life and death matters with fusty Sixties rhetoric about "pink triangles" and "final solutions." The political and public health establishments caved in to this rhetoric and, during crucial years when the virus first spread, stalled warnings that would have educated the gay public about the sexual transmission of AIDS (a fact which was originally, obdurately denied by leading gay activists). They denied the snowballing evidence that the epidemic was caused by reckless promiscuity and anal intercourse. (Even today, the words "promiscuous anal intercourse" are still censored out of the "education" literature that government agencies provide as the cornerstone of official anti-AIDS programs, because they are politically unacceptable to gay activists).

The attitudes struck and the policies adopted in San Francisco set the standard for the rest of the country. Gay leaders and the public health officials they so easily cowed refused to pursue strategies that might have slowed or even isolated the epidemic for fear they would infringe on a liberated lifestyle. Instead, with true Sixties gall, they indicted the government as "homophobic" for not providing more money for AIDS research. *America* was to blame. Ronald Reagan had somehow *caused*

---

[8]*Interview with Don Francis of the Center for Disease Control, Atlanta.*

AIDS by failing to mention it often enough. It was the sort of logic that might have been retrieved from a Sixties time capsule.

It is now too late for many of the public health measures that are a community's first line of defense against a virulent epidemic. The AIDs virus is in place and has now infected three-quarters of San Francisco's gay men and more than a million people nationwide. Other proven public health procedures like mandatory testing and contact tracing have been blocked by gay and liberal activists in the name of "civil rights." That it is in name only is clear from the phenomenon of "outing" practiced by radical gay groups themselves. The purpose of "outing" is to expose prominent gays still in the closet (a gay tabloid called *Outweek* provides the means). There has been no protest in the gay political community over this calculated invasion of privacy, despite the fact that protection of "confidentiality" is alleged as the primary reason for opposition to testing.

Meanwhile, the rhetorical excess continues. At the first national gay civil rights "March on Washington" attended by 200,000 activists in December 1987 as a reprise of King's moment in history, a prominent slogan proclaimed "Reagan No, Sodomy Yes" — as though anal sex had not been firmly established as one of the two principal modes of AIDS transmission, along with the sharing of needles. In a feature essay in the *Village Voice*, writer Richard Goldstein imbecilically described AIDS as the metaphor of the present generation in the way that Vietnam had been for the previous one and declared: "The sharing of needles must be understood in the same context as anal sex — as an ecstatic act that enhances social solidarity."

*   *   *

The same lesson about liberation can be learned from social epidemics as from venereal ones. The unprecedented increase in violent crimes that has infected America over the past two decades is an example. The Sixties defined itself by its efforts to delegitimize the police as an "army of occupation" while also celebrating crime as a form of existential rebellion and the outlaw as a perceptive social critic. There was a numbing barrage against what was derided as "law and order" seen in slogans such as "off the pigs," in the insistence that "all minority

prisoners are political prisoners," and in the romanticization of murderers like George Jackson who deserved to be locked deeper in the
prison system rather than becoming international symbols of American
injustice.

The Sixties raised incalculably what we now regard as an acceptable
level of violence and menace in our workaday existence — the crime
equivalent of Muzak murmuring in the background of our lives. Once
again, however, the most prominent victims were the intended
beneficiaries of this liberation — the black communities of the inner
cities who watch helplessly as crime tears their lives apart. But the social
theorists and Sixties nostalgia artists are as uncaring as they were for
those they delivered into the hands of the Communists in Vietnam.

And finally there is the Eighties drug epidemic, a delayed gift from
the Sixties and its ideology of consciousness expansion. For people like
Ken Kesey and Timothy Leary, drugs were the weapons of a folk
revolution, a democratization of the sublime, America in Wonderland.
For the political radicals, drugs were a shortcut to potentially revolutionary alienation and repudiation of the social mainstream. In 1969,
during the People's Park uprising in Berkeley, Tom Hayden and other
radicals drew up the "Berkeley Liberation Program" which, among other
things, promised to "protect and expand our drug culture..." and to
recognize "the right of people to use those drugs which are known from
experience to be harmful." Before the Movement's successes, drugs had
been quarantined in the social underground; now they had become part
of an individual's bill of rights. This moral imbecility stood out even in
the Sixties theater of the absurd. Yet the political ethos behind it survives
to this day. Thus, the *Nation*, a Leftist publication, recently condemned
Reagan's anti-drug policies as "an ideological mobilization like the war
against Communism... with its redolence of racism, its anti-Third World
and anti-Sixties overtones."

*   *   *

The nihilism that was part of the Sixties' advertisement for itself
makes it tempting to blame the decade for everything that has gone
wrong since. But to leave such an impression would, of course, be
uncharitable and untrue. There is a sense in which it *was* the best of

times. There *was* an expansion of consciousness, of social space, of tolerance, and of experience itself. It *was* exciting to be alive, to find oneself swimming in the rush of history's stream of consciousness. But while the beauty of the Sixties was that it was a decade of youth, its defect was an inability to grow up. It was constitutionally unable to see the other side of the ledger, condemned to ignore the fact that there are equal and opposite reactions in society as well as physics, social costs for social acts.

In the end, the words of Lennon decipher the truth of the era in a way that the works of the other Lenin, who enjoyed a brief but depressing vogue among radicals of the day, did not:

> You say you want a revolution?
> Well you know,
> We all want to change the world.
> You say you got a real solution?
> Well you know,
> We'd all love to see the plan.

But when all the posturing and self-dramatization was over, there was no plan, no idea about how to replace what had been destroyed.

Schizophrenic to its core, the era was never clear whether its primary identity was of creator or destroyer. Its ambivalence was suggested by the two groups that dominated the popular music which was the great, perhaps the only real artistic achievement of the time. Was the inner voice of the Sixties that of the Beatles, innocent minstrels on a "magical mystery tour?" Or the Rolling Stones, the vandals presiding at its "beggars' banquet?"

For a while, these groups reigned jointly over popular culture, expressing the audacious delusion of the Sixties that it was beyond consequences, beyond good and evil, able to have it all. It was possible to assault the cops by word and deed but also be safe on the streets, to reject authority and yet live coherently, to be an outlaw culture and yet a humane and harmoniously ordered one.

Listening to the Beatles and the Stones, Sixties rebels registered these ideas with growing grandiosity, believing they had gone from counter-culture to counter-nation once they planted the flag of discovery at Woodstock. A place consecrated by love, holy to the Sixties in the way the Paris commune was to the Marxist tradition, Woodstock institution-alized the right to live outside the rules. Unlike the doomed inhabitants of *Amerika*, the citizens of this new nation could have joyous copulation, access to illegal drugs. If the drugs caused bad trips or the sex carried disease, the caring immigrants of Woodstock would be there to care for their own.

But the Woodstock Nation was an illusion as ungrounded in reality as the hallucinations induced by the LSD which was its national chemical. A few months after its founding, the decade began to draw toward its apocalyptic close. As a portent of things to come, the Beatles were breaking up. The title song of the album might be taken as a recognition of the destructiveness of the Sixties crusade against the established order: *Let It Be*. The Rolling Stones answered this act of contrition with the title song of *their* album: *Let It Bleed*. Then came Altamont, the *Krystallnacht* of the Woodstock Nation. At Altamont, the gentle folk of Woodstock met the Hell's Angels — not only criminals but suppliers of the drugs which were destroying the new nation from within. While the Stones were singing *Sympathy for the Devil*, a black man lunged near the stage with a knife in his hand and was beaten to death in front of everyone by the Angels. Devils and Angels: it all came together and all came apart.

Appalled at what happened, Mick Jagger dropped the song from his repertory. He saw that the Sixties were over. It was time to go back to the dressing room, time to stop posturing as the "satanic majesties" of an era, time to grow up and simply become part of the rock scene again.

The rest of us had to do the same thing — learn to live with adulthood. And so the Sixties has faded into gauzy memory — the good old days when we were all so bad, a time of limitless possibilities and wild dreams made all the brighter by the somber and complex world which succeeded it. The paradoxical reason for the Sixties' growing appeal is this: it created the tawdry world which we now measure and find wanting by comparison to it.

There is truth in the nostalgia. It is the *memory* of the era that is false. The Pandora's Box the Sixties opened then is still unclosed; the malign influences released then still plague us today. □

Chapter Two

Goodbye To All That

(Peter Collier & David Horowitz)

When we tell our old radical friends that we voted for Ronald Reagan last November, the response is usually one of annoyed incredulity. After making sure that we are not putting them on, our old friends make nervous jokes about Jerry Falwell and Phyllis Schlafly, about gods that have failed, aging yuppies ascending to consumer heaven in their BMWs. We remind them of an old adage: "Anyone under 40 who isn't a socialist has no heart; anyone over 40 who is still a socialist has no brain." Inevitably the talk becomes bitter. One old comrade, after a tirade in which she denounced us as reactionaries and crypto-fascists, finally sputtered, "And the worst thing is that you've turned your back on the Sixties!" That was exactly right: casting our ballots for Ronald Reagan was indeed a way of finally saying good-bye to all that — to the self-aggrandizing romance with corrupt Third Worldism; to the casual indulgence of Soviet totalitarianism; to the hypocritical and self-dramatizing anti-Americanism which is the New Left's bequest to mainstream politics.

The instruments of popular culture may perhaps be forgiven for continuing to portray the Sixties as a time of infectious idealism, but those of us who were active then have no excuse for abetting this banality. If in some ways it was the best of times, it was also the worst of times, an era of bloodthirsty fantasies as well as spiritual ones. We ourselves experienced both aspects, serving as civil rights and antiwar activists and ending as co-editors of the radical magazine *Ramparts*. The magazine allowed us to write about the rough beast slouching through America and also to urge it on through non-editorial activities we

---

This article appeared as "Lefties for Reagan" in The Washington Post Magazine, *March 17, 1985. It has been edited for this volume.*

thought of as clandestine until we later read about them in the FBI and CIA files we both accumulated.

Like other radicals in those days, we were against electoral politics, regarding voting as one of those charades used by the ruling class to legitimate its power. We were even more against Reagan, then governor of California, having been roughed up by his troopers during the People's Park protests in Berkeley and tear-gassed by his National Guard helicopters during the University of California's Third World Liberation Front Strike. But neither elections nor elected officials seemed particularly important compared with the auguries of revolution the Left saw everywhere by the end of the decade — in the way the nefarious Richard Nixon was widening the war in Indochina; in the way unprovoked attacks were launched by paramilitary police against the Black Panther Party; in the formation of the Weather Underground, a group willing to pick up the gun or the bomb. It was a time when the apocalypse struggling to be born seemed to need only the slightest assist from the radical midwife.

When we were in the voting booth in 1984 (in different precincts but of the same mind) we both thought back to the day in 1969 when Tom Hayden came by the office and, after getting a *Ramparts* donation to buy gas masks and other combat issue for Black Panther "guerrillas," announced portentously: "Fascism is here, and we're all going to be in jail by the end of the year." We agreed wholeheartedly with this apocalyptic vision and in fact had just written in an editorial: "The system cannot be revitalized. It must be overthrown. As humanely as possible, but by any means necessary."

Every thought and perception in those days was filtered through the dark and distorting glass of the Vietnam war. The Left was hooked on Vietnam. It was an addictive drug whose rush was a potent mix of melodrama, self-importance and moral rectitude. Vietnam was a universal solvent — the explanation for every evil we saw and the justification for every excess we committed. Trashing the windows of merchants on the main streets of America seemed warranted by the notion that these petty bourgeois shopkeepers were cogs in the system of capitalist exploitation that was obliterating Vietnam. Fantasizing the death of local cops seemed warranted by the role they played as an occupying army in America's black ghettos, those mini-Vietnams we yearned to see explode in domestic wars of liberation. Vietnam caused us to support the extortionism and violence of groups like the Black Panthers, and dismiss derisively Martin Luther King Jr. as an "Uncle Tom."

How naive the New Left was can be debated, but by the end of the Sixties we were not political novices. We knew that bad news from Southeast Asia — the reports of bogged-down campaigns and the weekly body counts announced by Walter Cronkite — was good for the radical agenda. The more repressive our government in dealing with dissent at home, the more recruits for our cause and the sooner the appearance of the revolutionary Armageddon.

Our assumption that Vietnam would be the political and moral fulcrum by which we would tip this country toward revolution foresaw every possibility except one: that the United States would pull out. Never had we thought the United States, the arch-imperial power, would of its own volition withdraw from Indochina. This development violated a primary article of our hand-me-down Marxism: that political action through normal channels could not alter the course of the war. The system that we had wanted to overthrow worked tardily and only at great cost, but it worked.

When American troops finally came home, some of us took the occasion to begin a long and painful re-examination of our political assumptions and beliefs. Others did not. For the diehards, there was a post-Vietnam syndrome in its own way as debilitating as that suffered by people who had fought there — a sense of emptiness rather than exhilaration, a paradoxical desire to hold onto and breathe life back into the experience that had been their high for so many years. As the post-Vietnam decade progressed, the diehards on the Left ignored conclusions about the viability of democratic traditions that might have been drawn from America's exit from Vietnam and from the Watergate crisis that followed it, a time when the man whose ambitions they had feared most — Richard Nixon — was removed from office by the Constitution rather than by a coup.

The only "lessons" of Vietnam the Left seemed interested in were those that emphasized the danger of American power abroad and the need to diminish it, a view that was injected into the Democratic Party with the triumph of its McGovernite wing. The problem with this use of Vietnam as a moral text for American policy, however, was that the pages following the fall of Saigon had been whited out.

No lesson, for instance, was seen in Hanoi's ruthless conquest of the South, the establishment of a police state in Saigon and the political oblivion of the National Liberation Front, whose struggle we on the left had so passionately supported. It was not that credible information was lacking. Jean Lacouture wrote in 1976: "Never before have we had so much proof of so many detained after a war. Not in Madrid in 1939, not in Paris and Rome in 1944, nor in Havana in 1956... " But this eminent French journalist, who had been regarded as something of an oracle when he was reporting America's derelictions during the war, was now dismissed as a "sellout."

In 1977, when some former antiwar activists signed an Appeal to the Conscience of Vietnam because of the more than one million prisoners languishing in "re-education centers" and the new round of self-immolations by Buddhist monks, they were chastised by activist David Dellinger, Institute for Policy Studies fellow Richard Barnet and other keepers of the flame in a New York *Times* advertisement that said in part: "The present government of Vietnam should be hailed for its moderation and for its extraordinary effort to achieve reconciliation among all of its people." When tens of thousands of unreconciled "boat people" began to flee the repression of their Communist rulers, Joan Baez and others who spoke out in their behalf were attacked for breaking ranks with Hanoi.

Something might also have been learned from the fate of wretched Cambodia. But Leftists seemed so addicted to finding an American cause at the root of every problem that they couldn't recognize indigenous evils. As America was about to be defeated in Cambodia, radical theorist Noam Chomsky was heralding the coming of "a new era of economic development and social justice." The new era turned out to be the Communist killing fields that took the lives of two million Cambodians.

Finally, Vietnam emerged as an imperialistic power, seizing Laos and invading Cambodia (after its one-time proteges of the Khmer Rouge had

completed their work) in a bloody campaign whose immediate conse-
quence was the starvation of 350,000 more hapless Cambodian
peasants. The facts notwithstanding, a recent editorial in *The Nation*
explains that the Vietnamese invaded Cambodia "to stop the killing and
restore some semblance of civilized government to the devastated
country." This bloody occupation is actually a "rescue mission" and what
has happened should not "obscure the responsibility of the United States
for the disasters in Indochina," disasters that are being caused by playing
the "China card" and refusing to normalize relations with Vietnam.
These actions on the part of the United States "make Vietnamese
withdrawal from Cambodia unlikely"; only the White House can
"remove the pressures on Vietnam from all sides [that] would bring
peace to a ravaged land." Such reasoning recalls the wonderful line from
the Costa-Gavras film *Z*: "Always blame the Americans. Even when
you're wrong, you're right."

Another unacknowledged lesson from Indochina involves the way
in which Vietnam became a satellite of the Soviet Union (paying for
foreign aid by sending peasant labor brigades to its benefactor). This
development doesn't mesh well with the Left's ongoing romantic vision
of Hanoi. It also threatens the Left's obstinate refusal to admit that during
the mid-Seventies — a time when American democracy was trying to
heal itself from the twin traumas of the war and Watergate — the
U.S.S.R. was demonstrating that totalitarianism abhors a vacuum by
moving into Africa, Central America, Southeast Asia and elsewhere.
Instead of evaluating the Soviets' actions and intentions against the
change in what we used to call "the objective conditions" — specifically,
U.S. global withdrawal and paralysis after the defeat in Vietnam (an
opportunity which the Soviets obviously seized to expand their own
sphere), the Left rationalized Soviet aggression as the spasms of a
petrified bureaucracy, driven by fear of U.S. militarism, whose policies
are annoying mainly because they serve to distract attention from U.S.
malfeasance around the world.

If they had been capable of looking candidly at the Soviet empire,
Leftists and liberals alike would have to concur with Susan Sontag's
observation (which many of them jeered when she announced it) that
"Communism is fascism with a human face."

*   *   *

One of the reasons the Left was so cautious in its reassessments of the Soviets was the fiction that the U.S.S.R. in the early Eighties was on the side of "history." This assumption is echoed in Fred Halliday's euphoric claim, in a recent issue of *New Left Review*, that Soviet support was crucial to fourteen Third World revolutions since the fall of Saigon (including such triumphs of human progress as Iran and South Yemen), and in Andrew Kopkind's fatuous observation that "the Soviet Union has almost always sided with the revolutionists, the liberationists, the insurgents." In Ethiopia, for example? Propped up by 20,000 Cuban expeditionary forces, the Marxist government of Mengistu Haile Mariam had as its main accomplishment a "Red Campaign of Terror" (its official designation) that killed a hundred thousand intractable citizens, including virtually the entire 1977 graduating class of the high schools in Addis Ababba. Where were those who cheered the Soviets' work in behalf of the socialist *zeitgeist* when this episode took place? Or the following year, when Fidel Castro awarded Mengistu a "Bay of Pigs" medal — Cuba's highest honor — for this evil achievement? Or the fall of 1984 when the Marxist liberator squandered more than $40 million on a party celebrating the tenth anniversary of his murderous rule while his people starved? Where were they to point out the moral when capitalist America rushed in 250 million metric tons of grain to help allay the Ethiopian starvation?

Reagan was often upbraided for having described the Soviet Union as an evil empire. Those opposed to this term seemed to be offended aesthetically rather than politically. Just how wide of the mark was the President? Oppressing an array of nationalities whose populations outnumber its own, Russia was the last of the old European empires, keeping in subjugation not only formerly independent states such as Estonia, Latvia and Lithuania (Hitler's gift to Stalin), but also the nations of Eastern Europe. For seventy years, every country "liberated" into the Soviet bloc has been transformed into a national prison, where the borders are guarded to keep the inmates in rather than the foreigners out.

The war in Afghanistan was much more a metaphor for the Soviets' view of the world than Vietnam ever was for America's. Of the approximately 16 million people living in Afghanistan at the time of the Soviet invasion, an estimated 1 million were wounded and killed. There are now about 4 million refugees, a figure that does not include "internal" refugees — the hundreds of thousands of villagers forced to leave their scorched earth for the Soviet-controlled big cities, the only places where food is available. Or the thousands of Afghan children taken to the Soviet Union to be "educated," and who will eventually be returned to their native land as spies and quislings.

Soviet strategy in Afghanistan was based on a brutal rejoinder to Mao's poetic notion (which we old New Leftists used to enjoy citing) about guerrillas being like fish swimming in a sea of popular support. The Soviet solution was to boil the sea and ultimately drain it, leaving the fish exposed and gasping on barren land. The Soviet *blitzkrieg* is characterized by systematic destruction of crops and medical facilities, indiscriminate terror against the civilian populace, carpet bombings and the deadly "yellow rain" that even the leftist Peoples' Tribunal in Paris (successor to the Bertrand Russell War Crimes Tribunal) has said is being used in Afghanistan.

Throughout the early Eighties, during each December anniversary of the Soviet invasion, when liberal politicians rediscovered the *mujaheddin* guerrillas in the hills, after eleven months of moral amnesia, there were blithe references to Afghanistan as "Russia's Vietnam." Those who invoked the analogy seem to think that by simply doing so they have doomed the Russian storm troopers to defeat. But this analogy is based on a misunderstanding of what Vietnam was and what Afghanistan is. Unlike America's high-tech television war, Afghanistan was one of those old-fashioned encounters that take place in the dark. The Soviets made no attempts to win hearts and minds; the My Lais that were daily occurrences there caused no shock because they did not appear on Moscow TV; there were no scenes of the peasant children whose hands and faces were destroyed by antipersonnel bombs in the shape of toy trucks and butterflies witnesses saw strewn over the Afghan countryside; there were no images of body bags being offloaded from Soviet transports. Because there was no media coverage, there could be no growing revulsion on the home front, no protests on Soviet campuses and in Soviet streets, no clamor to bring the boys home.

Afghanistan was not Russia's Vietnam not only because the nation committing the atrocities never sees them, but because the rest of the world was blacked out, too. At the height of the Vietnam war there was a noncombatant army of foreign journalists present to witness its conduct. In Afghanistan they were forbidden, as were the Red Cross and all other international relief agencies that were integral to what happened in Vietnam. And without these witnesses, Afghanistan was a matter of "out of sight, out of mind."

The proper analogy for Afghanistan was not Vietnam at all but rather Spain — not in the nature of the war, but in the symbolic value it had — or should have — for our time. Aid to the *mujaheddin* should not have been a dirty little secret of the CIA, but a matter of public policy and national honor as well.

Perhaps the leading feature of the Left today is the moral selectivity that French social critic Jean-Francois Revel has identified as "the syndrome of the cross-eyed left." Leftists could describe Vietnam's conquest and colonization of Cambodia as a "rescue mission," while reviling Ronald Reagan for applying the same term to the Grenada operation, although better than 90 percent of the island's population told independent pollsters they were grateful for the arrival of U.S. troops. Forgetting for a moment that Afghanistan is "Russia's Vietnam," Leftists called Grenada "America's Afghanistan," although people in Afghanistan (as one member of the resistance there told us) would literally die for the elections held in Grenada.

* * *

The Left's memory can be as selective as its morality. When it comes to past commitments that have failed, the Leftist mentality is utterly unable to produce a coherent balance sheet. The attitude toward Soviet penetration of the Americas in the early Eighties was a good example. Enthusiasm for the Sandinista regime in Nicaragua should have recalled to those of us old enough to remember a previous enthusiasm for Cuba twenty-five years earlier. Many of us began our New Leftism with the Fair Play for Cuba demonstrations. We raised our voices and chanted, "*Cuba Si! Yanqui No!*" We embraced Fidel Castro not only because of the flamboyant personal style of the *barbudos* of his 26th of July Movement but also because Castro assured the world that his revolution belonged neither to Communists nor capitalists, that it was neither red nor black, but Cuban olive green.

We attributed Castro's expanding links with Moscow to the U.S.-sponsored invasion of the Bay of Pigs, and then to the "secret war" waged against Cuba by U.S. intelligence and paramilitary organizations. But while Castro's apologists in the United States may find it expedient to maintain these fictions, Carlos Franqui and other old Fidelistas now in exile have made it clear that Castro embraced the Soviets even before the U.S. hostility became decisive, and that he steered his country into an alliance with the Soviets with considerable enthusiasm. Before the Bay of Pigs he put a Soviet general in charge of Cuban forces. Before the Bay of Pigs he put Communists who had opposed the revolution in positions of power and destroyed Cuba's democratic trade unions, although their elected leadership was drawn from his own 26th of July movement. He did so because he knew that the Stalinists of Cuba's Communist Party would be dependable cheerleaders and efficient guardsmen of his emerging dictatorship.

One symbolic event along the way that many of us missed was Castro's imprisonment of his old comrade Huber Matos, liberator of Matanzas Province, and one of the four key military leaders of the revolution. Matos' crime: criticizing the growing influence of Cuban Communists (thereby jeopardizing Castro's plan to use them as his palace guard). Matos' sentence: twenty years in a 4-by-11 concrete box.

What has come of Cuba's revolution to break the chains of American imperialism? Soviets administer the still one-crop Cuban economy; Soviets train the Cuban army; and Soviet subsidies, fully one-quarter of Cuba's gross national product, prevent the Cuban treasury from going broke. Before the revolution, there were more than thirty-five independent newspapers and radio stations in Havana. Now, there is only the official voice of *Granma*, the Cuban *Pravda*, and a handful of other outlets spouting the same party line. In the mid-Eighties Cuba was a more abject and deformed colony of the Soviet empire than it ever was of America. The arch-rebel of our youth, Fidel Castro, had become a party hack who cheerfully endorsed the rape of Czechoslovakia in 1968 and endorses the ongoing plunder of Afghanistan today, an aging pimp who sold his young men to the Russians for use in their military adventures in return for $10 billion a year.

American Leftists still — even after the fall of Communism — propose solutions for the people of Central America that they wouldn't dare propose for themselves. These armchair revolutionaries project their self-hatred and their contempt for the privileges of democracy — which allow them to live well and think badly — onto people who would be only too grateful for the luxuries they disdain. Dismissing "bourgeois" rights as a decadent frill that the peoples of the Third World can't afford, Leftists spread-eagle the Central Americans between the dictators of the Right and the dictators of the Left. The latter, of course, are their chosen instruments for bringing social justice and economic well-being, although no Leftist revolutions have yet provided impressive returns on either of these promises, but have made the lives of their people considerably more wretched than they were before.

*   *   *

One of the few saving graces of age is a deeper perspective on the passions of youth. Looking back on the Left's revolutionary enthusiasms of the last twenty-five years, we have painfully learned what should have been obvious all along: that we live in an imperfect world that is bettered only with great difficulty and easily made worse — much worse. This is a conservative assessment, but on the basis of half a lifetime's experience, it seems just about right. □

Chapter Three

Three Myths About the Sixties

(*Peter Collier*)

While the Sixties, that age of wonders, is over in fact, it is still with us in spirit. Nostalgia artists have made it into a holograph that creates beguiling images of the last good time — a prelapsarian age of good sex, good drugs, and good vibes. For unreconstructed Leftists, the Sixties is not just an era of good fun but of good politics — a time of monumental idealism populated by individuals who wanted nothing more than to give peace a chance; a time of commitment and action when young people in the throes of moral passion sought to remake the world.

Three myths have served to deform the memory of the Sixties, to conjure the false images of idealism and innocence, and to hide the realities of a destructive generation.

The first is that the goal of the Sixties Left was to make America a better democracy. Jim Miller is one of the purveyors of this myth. His book *Democracy Is In The Streets* focuses on the Movement code words "participatory democracy," and takes its title from a misconstrued slogan of the times. Miller perpetuates as history the false impression we radicals set out to create for tactical reasons: that a better, more liberal democracy was what the New Left wanted.

This was true in the sense that, like radicals before us, we had a fantasy about a future that *was* perfectly democratic and just, and therefore so irresistibly attractive that it would justify our real purpose which — as Marxist radicals — was to destroy the only democratic society we had known. But in contrast to the rhetorical smokescreen that we consciously created, the practical, immediate meaning of the slogan "Democracy is in the Streets" to us, as the Sixties began, was that

---

Speech given in Cambridge, March 23, 1989.

the two-party system in America was a sham designed to protect the power monopoly of the corporate rulers; that "bourgeois democracy" was merely an instrument of class oppression; that the task of the revolutionary was to tear the liberal mask from the tyrant's face, to lead the gullible citizenry out of the polling booths and into the streets; to bring the system down; to destroy, in short, the existing institutions and authorities of democratic America, in order to replace them with the Marxist totalitarian fantasy that we embraced with our hearts. This is what we were prepared to do; this is what we did.

Like other recent books by self-serving nostalgia artists, Miller's account conceals as much as it reveals of the intentions of the time. In his version, New Leftists set out to create a "participatory democracy" but were misled by "breakaway experiences" along the way — moments in which real boundaries "melted...and it seemed as if anything could happen,...moments...when people...sensed...that together they could change the world." In Miller's account, the headlong descent of the Movement into cultural malice and political mayhem up to and including its ultimate collusion with totalitarian evil was the result not of any malign intention or original sin, but rather an excess of innocence, a luxuriant idealism whose intoxicating vapors robbed it of its senses: "In the mounting enthusiasm for 'breakaway experiences' the original vision of democracy was all but forgotten. The spirit of ecstatic freedom proved impossible to sustain. The Movement collapsed..." In this political vacuum, writes Miller, "frustrated revolutionists built bombs, turning reveries of freedom into cruel ineffectual outbursts of terrorism. And one by one, the political pilgrims who had created 'the Sixties' fell back to earth." Thus Miller restores to the Sixties its own narcissistic self-image as a time of saints.

In fact, "breakaway experiences" did not give us the sense that together we might change the world. That was our *premise*. That was what made us radicals — and not just liberal Democrats — to begin with. "Participatory democracy" was not a freshly discovered concept, but a new liberal code for an old Marxist idea. With one significant exception — I will come to him in a moment — the New Leftists who coined it were children of Communists or members of the Marxisant Left, and I remember hearing it in Berkeley and instantly recognizing it as an Americanized version of "Soviet" — as in Lenin's slogan "All power to the Soviets!" This was a post-McCarthy America and a post-Khrush-chev world. We were New Left because we could not be Old Left. We wanted to restore the original bloom to the Bolshevik Revolution that had been perverted, the Soviet democracy that Stalin had destroyed. The phrase "participatory democracy" served two essential political ends: it revived a pure revolutionary faith; it formulated an alien agenda in domestically acceptable terms.

There is this truth, then, in the image of our idealism. It is the fatuous hope that we could rescue Communism from its bloody self, that we could make the revolutionary future different this time. But there was a deeper malevolence — we called it *alienation* — which was this: that we chose the path of revolution, which meant that we embraced war by any means necessary against the System, the only real democracy we knew.

The non-Marxist architect of SDS was Tom Hayden. Hayden had the malevolent hostility required to be a revolutionary, but he didn't quite have the faith. By his own account, Hayden had acquired the faith by the winter of 1965, when he accepted the invitation of Herbert Aptheker — one of the most despicable hacks in the annals of American Communism — to spend two weeks in Communist North Vietnam. There he found the perfect model for the participatory democracy he and the other SDS founders had been talking about. In a book, written on his return, he described the "constant dialogue" encouraged by Communist guerrillas in village meetings, which he and his co-author Staughton Lynd called "rice-roots democracy." They said: "We suspect that colonial American town meetings and current Vietnamese village meetings, Asian peasants' leagues and Black Belt sharecroppers' unions have much in common." They described the Stalinist Communism of North Vietnam as a "socialism of the heart."

This is the original sin of the Sixties movement: that its intentions were Marxist and revolutionary, and therefore malevolent — anti-American and anti-democratic — from the start. The bad conclusion was already present in the innocent seeming premise. Just as it is in the rainbow of Lefts that confront us today. All the other myths about the Sixties Left flow from the failure to acknowledge this fact.

The second myth is that the New Left was a movement for civil rights or — as Miller puts it — "for the dignity of American blacks." There is a superficial truth in this claim too. The New Left was for civil rights in the way that Lenin's Bolsheviks were for land, bread and peace: as a tactical means to a strategic end. The strategic end for the New Left was not civil rights for American blacks but the destruction of the "corporate liberal" American system. By 1965 when Tom Hayden had discovered a soulful socialism of the heart in Communist Vietnam, the civil rights movement had won a tremendous historic victory. Legal segregation in America was history; for the first time since the birth of the Republic, black Americans had been made full citizens before the law. It was a triumph of the American system. But the New Left did not even pause to celebrate. Instead, at this very moment the New Left went on the attack, proclaiming "black power" and "black liberation," and ridiculing integrationists like Martin Luther King. Blacks, in this New Left vision, were victims not only of discrimination and prejudice but of the American empire itself, of Amerika spelled with a "k." They could only be liberated by the destruction of the liberal values and institutions that oppressed them.

Of all the poisonous vapors we continue to inhale from the swamp of the Sixties, this is surely the most pernicious. Today the poisons of racism — of discriminatory double standards and legally enforced prejudice — are progressive passions. Martin Luther King's dream of equal opportunity — of every person judged by the content of their character — is a rearguard conservative cause.

The last and most mendacious myth about the Left of the Sixties is that it was an anti-war movement. It was, in fact, a movement that wanted the Communists to win. And America to lose. Thus in 1965, when SDS confronted the war and peace issue, it instantaneously rejected Paul Potter's genuine anti-war slogan of "Burn not, build" and substituted the destructive and self-exposing cry: "Burn. Not Build." In the end, the Sixties Left got what it wanted: the Communists won and America lost. And therefore the poor of Vietnam and Indochina lost too. And not only in Southeast Asia, but in Afghanistan, and Ethiopia and Central America, where the Communist expansion encouraged by America's defeat in Vietnam exacted terrible tolls as well.

The Left is not about peace; it is about war. Permanent war against the democratic society in which we live. And this is its authentic voice, which I quote from a page of *New Left Notes*, the official organ of SDS:

> You have to realize that the issue didn't matter. The issues were never the issues. You could have been involved with the Panthers, the Weatherpeople, SLATE, SNCC, SDS. It didn't really matter what. It was the revolution that was everything... That's why dope was good. Anything that undermined the system contributed to the revolution and was therefore good.

The Left today is still high on revolutionary destruction and still has no plan. The dream is over: Socialism is dead. It is not — and never was — a redemptive future, only a hellish past. The Left is not the vanguard of a progressive idealism, but a reactionary nihilism, socially destructive, and morally corrupt. It is not for civil rights for America's communities, but only for civil war. It is not anti-interventionist, or for human rights, or for peace in the hemisphere's fratricidal conflicts: in El Salvador, it still wants the Communists to win.

It is time now for the radical warriors of our generation to take a real look at the virtues of the democratic America on which they have for so long made war, to reckon up the awful damage and the destructive consequences their warfare has entailed, to accept the amnesty that only so generous a democracy can offer, and to gather up the courage to finally come home. ☐

Chapter Four

AIDS: The Origins of a Political Epidemic

(Peter Collier & David Horowitz)

Liberty Baths may have the look of a sexual YMCA — showers and a sauna, hair dryers, Coke machines, and gay men cruising the halls with towels wrapped around their waists — but it is actually part of a medical and political controversy over a sexually transmitted disease that is tearing San Francisco apart. In the basement are scores of private rooms with muffled sounds of ecstasy coming from behind closed doors. One door is open, and a man lies facedown on a cot presenting himself seductively to anyone who might happen by. On the top floor is a carpeted viewing room where naked men watch gay porn on a movie screen while idly fondling each other. Down the hall a middle-aged man stands at one of the stalls that have "glory holes" cut in at waist level while a faceless stranger on the other side of the partition performs *fellatio* on him.

The only place where there seems to be conversation is at the lunch counter, where two naked men are munching on hamburgers and talking about the AIDS epidemic that has begun to terrify the city. "I could get back into the closet right now," says one of the men, "and still get it in a year or so. So what would I have achieved? Celibacy?" The other nods enthusiastically. "I know," he says. "We're just little time bombs, aren't we?" Then he stands, stretches, and wipes his mouth with a napkin. "Well, I don't know about you, but I'm going to have some

This article appeared in California Magazine, *in July 1983, just as AIDS was breaking into the public consciousness and before the HIV virus was isolated and identified as a cause. There were only 1,500 confirmed cases nationwide, compared to more than 170,000 today. What are now obvious truths regarding the spread of AIDs were, in 1983, regarded as "homophobia" on the part of the authors.* California Magazine *was picketed by gay activists after the article appeared.*

fun while I *tick*." After they have gone, the short-order cook shakes his head. "Did you hear that? It's like some straight joke about queers."

The humor *has* gotten grimmer in San Francisco. ("How does Anita Bryant spell relief?" goes one of the sicker jokes. "A-I-D-S.") And beneath this brittle bravado, the city exhibits the signs of profound anxiety and turmoil. Police requisition latex masks and surgical gloves when they have to deal with gays; gay landlords evict tenants showing the telltale purple lesions of Kaposi's sarcoma, a rare skin cancer associated with AIDS; patrons worry about frequenting the city's restaurants, where many of the service workers are gay; health workers who do not hesitate to deal with most grotesque street maladies treat hospitalized AIDS patients like lepers, shunting them off in remote rooms and sometimes allowing buttons to go unanswered.

It might be expected that the very organized and most powerful gay political machine in the country would have been able to deal with this situation. And in a limited way it has. Led by San Francisco's only gay supervisor, Harry Britt, and supported by Mayor Dianne Feinstein, the San Francisco Board of Supervisors appropriated $4 million for the present fiscal year to combat AIDS, and the congressional offices of the late Phillip Burton (Democrat, San Francisco) and Barbara Boxer (Democrat, Marin County) have rigorously lobbied Washington for more money. But for the most part, gay leaders have resolutely, and astonishingly, refused to speak out on the basic issue of AIDS — the medical consensus that it is contracted and spread through sexual contact — and they have failed to demand the prophylactic measures that could help contain the disease.

Recognizing this as an issue that threatens the political momentum that could lead to gay control of the board of supervisors within the next decade, gay leaders have made the matter of AIDS transmission into a "dirty little secret." As a result of their influence, until May of this year there was not a single piece of health department literature in the city's health clinics to inform their high-risk clientele of the fact that AIDS is transmitted through blood and semen. Public health officials have suppressed information about the extent of the epidemic. Attempts to close places such as the gay baths, where the anonymous public sex implicated in the spread of the disease takes place, have been preemptively crushed. And those gay public figures who have tried to provoke a discussion of the issues have often felt pressure and intimidation.

Catherine Cusic is a lesbian who heads the Gay/Lesbian Health Services Committee of the Harvey Milk Gay Democratic Club's AIDS Task Force. She is outraged by the dereliction of the gay leadership. "It is a pattern that goes back to the first appearance of AIDS," she says. "There are leaders in this community who don't want people to know the truth. Their attitude is that it is bad for business, bad for the gay image. Hundreds, perhaps thousands, are going to die because of this attitude. The whole thing borders on the homicidal."

As the medical community has worked to isolate and identify the virus it now feels certain causes AIDS, there has been a parallel struggle to define the disease socially. Some of the most violent talk has come from Christian fundamentalists, who compare AIDS to a biblical plague, and from secular moralists, who use the ready-made metaphor of Mother Nature finally striking back at transgressors against her laws. Gays, too, have been guilty of rhetorical excess. This may be understandable, given the history of discrimination and oppression from which they have so recently emerged. Carelessly using terms such as "genocide" and "holocaust," they view the slow progress of medical research as evidence of homophobia and compare it with the quick response to Legionnaires' Disease and Toxic Shock Syndrome. The AIDS virus just happens to have struck the gay community first, they say, and could just as easily have had its malignant genesis in the heterosexual world.

In fact, the federal health bureaucracy has reacted forthrightly, if not especially swiftly, as AIDS has attained the critical mass necessary to make it a significant national health issue. Dr. Edward Brandt, assistant secretary of the U.S. Health and Human Services Department, has identified the disease as the "number-one priority" for the U.S. Public Health Service. In May, Congress moved to appropriate $12 million to fight the epidemic, which would bring the total federal expenditures to $26 million — considerably more than was spent battling either Legionnaires' Disease or Toxic Shock Syndrome over a longer period of time.

Gay leaders have reacted by charging that this money represents the tardy cynicism of a society worried that AIDS will jump the boundaries of the gay world and become a general menace. In fact, the disease has affected three narrowly defined high-risk groups in addition to bisexuals and gays with multiple partners: drug addicts, hemophiliacs, and Haitians. Moreover, while heterosexuals have been affected, there has often been a link to homosexuality: drug users sometimes share needles with gays; hemophiliacs receive blood from gay donors; and, according to Haitian officials, more than 30 percent of the victims in that country are homosexuals. In California, particularly, the epidemic has imploded on gays, who constitute at least 90 percent of AIDS victims. Because the disease is communicable, spreading as a result of sexual contact, the only way in which the analogy with Legionnaires' Disease or Toxic Shock Syndrome would hold is if the Legionnaires had insisted on returning to the hotel where they contracted their malady or if women had continued to use the dangerous tampons.

Columnist Herb Caen was one of the first to alert San Francisco to the confusion and schisms within the gay community. In late May he reported in the *San Francisco Chronicle* that a gay doctor had run into three of his AIDS patients in one of the baths and ordered them out, only to have them refuse to leave and threaten to sue him for breach of confidentiality. But the gay community's ambivalence in facing up to the disease is nothing new. Several months ago, Catherine Cusic asked the city's public health department to put up posters about AIDS on buses and in other public places. The suggestion was presented to Pat Norman, a lesbian who coordinates the city's lesbian-gay health services, but no action was taken. Since then, while more and more gays have contracted AIDS, the department has maintained a curiously uninvolved stance. Most public health experts, including gays, have come to the conclusion that the disease is sexually transmitted and that unprotected anal intercourse significantly increases the risk. "The agent is probably a blood-borne virus in many ways similar to hepatitis B, which can be transmitted by direct inoculation of blood and through intimate sexual contact...where bleeding takes place," said Dr. Marcus Conant, who works with the gay-run Kaposi's Sarcoma/AIDS Foundation, at a recent city-sponsored AIDS symposium. However, in a pamphlet prepared by the foundation and distributed by the city, references to anal sex or any sex connected with trauma were omitted.

Cusic and other members of her committee have come to regard all this as a "conspiracy of silence," although at times it seems more to resemble a campaign of disinformation with clear political overtones. They point out that Pat Norman and the gay health activists who support her in the moderate Alice B. Toklas Memorial Democratic Club, a gay organization, have ties to the mayor's office and to political patronage. And the Toklas club apparently fears that taking a stand on the issue of the transmission of AIDS will cause a backlash against the city's institutionalized gay life-style and against gay businesses, which have become an important aspect of San Francisco's economy. When the Harvey Milk club recently joined a recall campaign against Mayor Feinstein, the Toklas club backed the mayor (who herself worried that the AIDS scare might keep the city from becoming a site for the 1984 Democratic Convention).

The politics involved in AIDS are not only intramural and civic but sexual as well. The philosophy of the Stonewall Gay Democratic Club is "Sex doesn't cause AIDS — a virus does." This has become the rallying cry of gays who fear the hidden message inherent in acknowledging that the disease is sexually transmitted: physician, heal thyself. In the words of one gay leader, "[People] worried that if they admitted the disease was spread sexually, everything that had been said about their lifestyle would seem true. They just wouldn't admit it, whatever the evidence."

The extent of this willingness to suppress information became clear earlier this year. Andrew Moss and Michael Gorman, two researchers at UC San Francisco Medical Center, completed a study showing that 1 of every 333 single men in the Castro area (including Noe Valley and the Haight) had already been diagnosed as having AIDS. On January 16 and on several occasions over the following weeks, Moss and Gorman met with gay health activists from the Kaposi Sarcoma/AIDS Foundation, the Bay Area Physicians for Human Rights, the three gay Democratic clubs, and public health officials to discuss their findings. Despite some dissent, however, the consensus at these meetings was against making the Moss-Gorman figures public, lest they be "misinterpreted."

At a meeting in early March to draft a statement on AIDS for the Lesbian/Gay Freedom Day Parade, Bill Kraus, an aide to the late Congressman Phil Burton, and Dana Van Gorder, of Supervisor Britt's office, strongly urged inclusion of the Moss-Gorman findings. Their proposal was defeated by Pat Norman and the other committee members, and the report languished until later that month, when it was leaked to Randy Shilts, a reporter on the *Chronicle's* gay beat. Public health director Mervyn Silverman now says, "It didn't tell us anything we didn't already know." But he admits that he never saw the study, which was held back by health department officials. "There was never a decision that it should not be put out," Norman says, echoing Moss and Gorman's point of view, "but a question as to what context it should be put out in." Dr. Selma Dritz, assistant director of the health department's communicable disease division and a collaborator on the report, did not push the study, either. She says that the decision of whether or not to publish was up to Moss and Gorman.

Explaining his decision to publish the report, Shilts — who is gay — says, "The people in the Castro had a right to know this. If they're tricking in the bars, they've got a real good chance of tricking with somebody who has the disease. I got a call from Gorman, telling me not to print the information. Gay political leaders called, including Randy Stallings [president of the Toklas club and co-chair with Norman of the Coalition for Human Rights, the umbrella organization for all the gay groups in San Francisco]. In eight years as a journalist, I've never been under such pressure to suppress a story. People kept telling me it would hurt business in the Castro, hurt the Gay Rights Bill in Sacramento. My feeling is, what the hell, if you're dead, what does the rest of it matter?"

Other gay leaders who had been pushing to get the conclusions of the Moss-Gorman study publicized and acted upon also found themselves under pressure. One of them was Kraus. "I kept saying that people have a right to know this," he says. "Those who wanted to keep the report under wraps said that if it got out, people would be afraid to come to the Castro, that AIDS patients would be thrown out of restaurants and all that. I went through an agonizing period saying to myself, 'What the hell is going on here? How can these people do this? How can they try to suppress this data?' It's still not entirely clear to me why they did it, but I do know how. They intimidate people into silence by saying that they're homophobic, anti-sex, and all kinds of other things people don't want to be called."

Ironically, during the time that this debate was going on, 68 new cases of AIDS were reported. The connection between promiscuous sex and AIDS was by now so obvious to some gays that they had started masturbation clubs, were seeking more stable relationships, and had begun to criticize those who were spreading the disease. "We Know Who We Are," an article by Michael Callen and Richard Berkowitz, two gays who have AIDS, was circulating in something like *samizdat* form before finally being printed by the Sacramento gay newspaper *Mom...Guess What!* They cited medical evidence that gays are particularly susceptible to the disease because of repeated shocks to their immune systems caused by treatment for other sexually transmitted diseases, and concluded that gays must take personal responsibility for their condition. "The present epidemic of AIDS among promiscuous urban gay males is occurring because of the unprecedented promiscuity of the last ten to fifteen years," they wrote. "The commercialization of promiscuity and the explosion of establishments such as bathhouses, bookstores, and backrooms is unique in Western history. It has been mass participation in this lifestyle that has led to the creation of an increasingly disease-polluted pool of sexual partners."

Yet, while there were individual efforts to try to control the disease, there was not enough support to make it a majority movement. In a study conducted early this year, three gay psychotherapists — Leon McKusick, William Horstman, and Arthur Carfagni — compiled questionnaire responses from 600 gay men and concluded that, while fears about AIDS were increasing and some modification of sexual activity had occurred, an alarming number of men were still engaging in high-risk behavior. An article about this study in the *Bay Area Reporter*, a leading gay paper, said that a large proportion of those interviewed were "continuing to engage in behavior that could transmit an AIDS infective agent — and at the same frequency as before they found out about AIDS." Perhaps most devastating of all was the finding that "the gay men surveyed are still poorly informed about the disease transmission or are unwilling or unable to change sexual patterns."

The Lesbian/Gay Freedom Day march, scheduled for June 26, presented an opportunity for some remedial education, but also for disaster. An estimated 300,000 gays from all over the United States would be coming to San Francisco and could spread the disease to uninfected gay communities throughout the country, especially if they patronized the city's bathhouses, which feature precisely the kind of sex most likely to spread AIDS. On May 24 the Harvey Milk club met and finally voted 80-1 to put out a pamphlet warning of the sexual trans-mission of the disease. Members of the club, among them congressional aide Bill Kraus, also joined with other concerned gay leaders to try to persuade bathhouse owners to dispense condoms and post warnings that oral and anal sex greatly increase the chances of contracting the disease. Kraus recalls that "not only were the bathhouse owners totally incensed that we'd suggest that they do something, but the Toklas club made a statement saying that what we were proposing did not represent their policy. We wound up on the defensive, spending our time explain-ing how we weren't really breaking ranks, et cetera, et cetera."

In desperation, Kraus joined with Cleve Jones, a gay aide to San Francisco assemblyman Art Agnos, and with Ron Huberman, of the Harvey Milk club, and wrote a manifesto that was printed — after editor Paul Lorch sat on it for six weeks — in the *Bay Area Reporter*. "What a peculiar perversion it is of gay liberation to ignore the overwhelming scientific evidence, to keep quiet, to deny the obvious — when the lives of gay men are at stake," they wrote. "What a strange concept of our gay movement it is to care more about what they may do to us than about the need to spread the news about this disease to our people so that we can protect each other." The letter convinced Supervisor Harry Britt to take a stand on the bathhouse issue. "I didn't think he'd have the guts to do it," says Randy Shilts. "But after Kraus, Jones, and Huberman published their letter, he finally saw that this was the side to be on and said in effect that we can't keep on humping like bunnies."

Others, however, saw the letter as treason to the gay cause. With the sophistry that was coming to dominate the debate, Toklas club president Randy Stallings wrote in a letter in the *Bay Area Reporter*: "No one knows what causes AIDS or how it is transmitted, but one thing is certain. If this illness is sexually transmitted, it can be transmitted from someone met in church as easily as someone met at a bathhouse. To single out one type of gay business as somehow 'responsible' for the epidemic is to begin the process of destroying our community... Labeling San Francisco as unsafe for our people is inaccurate and a direct attack on the social and economic viability of our community."

But others tried to get Health Director Mervyn Silverman to close the bathhouses for the parade weekend. The public health director's response was, "It is not the bathhouses that are the problem — it's sex. People who want to have sex will find a way to have it." Shilts points out the consequences of such logic: "If one guy has sex with ten guys in a night — and some do — the risk becomes 1 in 33 for this guy. And he can take his dormant case of AIDS back to Iowa or wherever and start it going there." And Shilts sees an ultimate irony in all this: "People organizing the march want large numbers so they can have a show of force to press the federal government on AIDS research."

Shilts got so upset by the posturing and procrastination that he spent a day lobbying the board of supervisors and the mayor, eventually securing a commitment that literature specifying the risks of bathhouse sex would be distributed to patrons. At first Silverman denied that he had the authority to enforce such a request. However, Mayor Feinstein (who was on the verge of signing sweeping legislation regulating smoking in the workplace) quoted to him the article of the city code giving him the power to act. Finally Silverman met with bathhouse owners in a new mood of realism. "Their businesses are likely to be affected if people keep dying from this damned thing," he said. "It is in everybody's interest   through altruism and humanitarianism, but also capitalism — to get this thing taken care of."

Privately, many gay spokesmen claim that they would like to see the bathhouses closed altogether. They worry about the conclusion that can be drawn from the spread of AIDS — that homosexuality can be hazardous to one's health. But some activists insist that the bathhouses must be defended precisely because they are the center of the most extreme form of public gay sexual behavior. And so the bathhouses have become a perverse and inchoate symbol of gay liberation itself.

Gay freedom parade co-chairman Konstantin Berlandt is a former editor of UC Berkeley's *Daily Californian* and antiwar activist. He sees the proposals to close the bathhouses as "genocidal" and compares them to the order requiring homosexuals to wear triangular pink shirt patches in Nazi Germany. Berlandt wrote a *Bay Area Reporter* account of the first closed meeting of concerned gays and bathhouse owners, which was widely credited with torpedoing the effort to get them to inform patrons that they were at risk. "We fought Anita Bryant and John Briggs [anti-homosexual crusaders], and we'll fight against AIDS. Every time the community has been attacked the parades have been larger," he says, defending his opposition to the warning. "You have a situation where institutions that have fought against sexual repression for years are being attacked under the guise of medical strategy." Despite mounting medical evidence, Berlandt believes that transmission of the disease via bodily fluids is nothing more than a "theory" being used to attack the gay lifestyle. "I haven't stopped having sex," he says. "I feel that what we're being advised to do involves all the things I became gay to get away from — wear a condom, that sort of thing. So we have a disease for which supposedly the cure is to go back to all the styles that were preached at us in the first place. It will take a lot more evidence before I'm about to do that."

For gays who have worked hard and, so far, unsuccessfully to get the community to face up to the consequences of AIDS — to its symbolism and its reality — such a statement represents denial at an elemental level. It is an inability to admit the magnitude of what is unfolding and an inability to accept responsibility for the role that personal excess has played in this health crisis. It also represents a mentality that insists on making a political and ideological argument out of what remains, above all, a personal tragedy.

Catherine Cusic, in addition to working with the Harvey Milk club's health services committee, is a respiratory therapist at San Francisco General Hospital. What she sees there in the intensive care unit gives her a perspective that gay politicians and ideologues do not have. "It's my job to take care of patients unable to breathe on their own, without the help of a machine — in other words, the dying AIDS patients," she says. "You see these young people come in and die so quickly and in such agony. Their family comes in and watches. It's terrible when parents outlive their children. In some sense what I witness is political for me. I say to myself, 'We're queers. They don't care about us. They're glad we're dying.' But it's also personal. I watch these young men die. Their mothers start to cry. Their lovers have been sitting in the room, smiling and smiling, and then I see them at the elevator just standing and sobbing. It's horrible. And it's a horrible death. The patients waste away until they look like Dachau victims in the end. I see all this happen, and

I have to admit that some of those responsible are gay leaders. In my mind they're criminally negligent. They've betrayed their own community." □

Chapter Five

Tom & Jane & Whittaker & Alger

(Peter Collier)

The topic of the evening is Hollywood and Hollywood politics, and I guess I should begin by establishing my authority to make any judgments about this place, the outer isles of the American imagination. I was born in Hollywood Presbyterian Hospital almost exactly fifty years ago. It was a time when any boy could grow up to be President or, even better, to be in the movies. When I was five my mother took me for a screen test. It was at a place out in the San Fernando Valley where they were shooting a western. They were looking for a boy to play a featured role. I was apparently acquitting myself well in the intake interview, when a majestic palomino that looked like Roy Rogers' horse suddenly passed by. I said, "Jesus, Mom, it's Trigger!" and ran off after it. The talent scout told my mother that a child star had to be disciplined and obedient, and that Hollywood didn't tolerate profanity. So that was that.

Still, being in Hollywood, we grew up on the edges of the industry, going to previews and private screenings, and always star-gazing. But it wasn't until I was in high school, at the end of the Fifties, that movies began to speak to me with the intimate feel of revelation. James Dean and Marlon Brando embodied my inchoate dreams in a fundamental way — in who they were, or seemed to be, as well as in the characters they played. I think the first political thought I ever had came from "The Wild Ones," in which Brando plays the head of a motorcycle gang that terrorizes some small California town, probably Hollister. At one point during the rampage, the embattled mayor comes up to Brando and says something like, "What's wrong? What is it you people are rebelling against?" You all remember what happens next. Brando looks at him laconically and replies, "I don't know, what have you got?"

Speech given before the Pumpkin Papers Irregulars, October 31, 1989.

I was surprised later on to discover that more than a few people I got to know in the New Left also regarded this as a prestige moment. What were we rebelling against? We don't know, what have you got? Soon after I got to Berkeley in 1959, I realized that this could become the punch line for a generation. It was our version of *cogito ergo sum*. I am against therefore I am.

This idea of rebellion without a cause, of acting out on a grand scale, spoke to half of what became the New Left. My half. Not my friend David Horowitz's half. The red diaper babies, Communists without a cause because of Stalin, were far more important in the movement than Sixties historians — those nostalgia artists who defend the golden realm — like to admit. But they wouldn't have gotten anywhere without us, without the do-it group, the fans of Dean and Brando, afficianados of existentialism and authenticity, of the *acte gratuit*. Without us they would have sat around during the Sixties trying to figure out how to get Herbert Aptheker's books published by Random House and how to infiltrate the Democratic Party and how to get Paul Robeson to sing "Old Man River" on baseball's opening day. Well, at least they can say they're one for three after all these years.

Of course, without the Communists of the New Left, we never would have known about the labor theory of value. These red diaper babies knew about Marx. But my half of the New Left knew about movies. We knew about denouements. We knew about transitions. (The Communists' idea of a smooth transition is shown by the errata sheet Khrushchev ordered up for the *Soviet Encyclopedia* after the KGB Chief Lavrenti Beria had been liquidated — "for Beria substitute Bering Straits"). We realized that the New Left had to have high drama to hold onto its easily distracted members and to capture the imagination of the country. It is probably no accident that so many of the Movement's events had a filmic quality. The Black Panthers engaging in a series of bloody shootouts with the police in 1968 was film *noir*. The Weatherman cult blowing itself up in the townhouse explosion a year or so later was *cinema verite*. Anything involving Abbie Hoffman was the Three Stooges. (Not to speak ill of the dead, but he was all the Stooges rolled into one — the Larry, Daryl and Daryl of the New Left.)

We were always wary of being "coopted" by Hollywood. And when Hollywood came to the Movement these fears proved well founded. Hollywood's idea was to turn Stanley Kramer loose on New Left themes, or even worse, Michelangelo Antonioni, whose *Zabriskie Point* showed actual Berkeley radicals like Eldridge Cleaver's wife Kathleen having a rap session! But then something portentous happened: Hollywood stopped trying to make films *about* the Left and instead became *part* of the Left.

I think I know the moment — if not the exact moment, then a proximate one — when this happened. It was December 1969. I had just written a story for *Ramparts Magazine* about the Indian occupation of Alcatraz. I got a call from Jane Fonda. She was in India, where she had gone, following the Beatles lead, to do meditation with the Mahareshi after breaking up with her French director husband Roger Vadim. She told me that she was sick of living in exile and told me she wanted to come home and get involved in the New Left. She asked if I would show her around the Movement and get her involved. Of course I said I would. Not long afterwards she showed up in San Francisco and said take me to Alcatraz. Naturally, I said okay.

It was an odd experience. Within minutes she had felt out the power arrangements on the island and seen that there was a turf struggle going on between the Navajos and the Sioux and seen too that the Sioux were more radical. When I left her late in the day, she was in the cellblock of the old prison where some of the self-styled Sioux warriors hung out. She was smoking dope with them and learning what they told her was a war chant.

After that she was on her way. Jane was a quick study, picking up immediately on the Movement lingo it had taken the rest of us a decade to develop. I got a couple of letters from her. They were written in a backhanded scrawl and the closing salutation was "all power to the people!" There was an exclamation point after the word "people." The thing that intrigued me was that when she made an exclamation point the dot was actually a little circle instead of a dot. My wife, who was probably jealous of my "relationship" with Jane, took one look at this circle and said, "I'm surprised she didn't make it into a smiley face."

Now and then I caught glimpses of Jane as she ascended quickly into the upper reaches of the Left. I remember particularly an appearance on the Dick Cavett Show. This was when she was a couple with Mark Lane, who had gotten his start as a radical with his theories about the Kennedy assassination and taken that same intellectual acuity into his activism against the war in Vietnam. Lane had given Jane the rudiments of a Marxist critique of the war, which was just then replacing the critique based on moral outrage. Cavett asked Jane how she thought we had gotten involved in Vietnam. She replied that it happened because Eisenhower wanted a monopoly of the "tung and tinsten" of Southeast Asia. I stored the Spoonerism up in a memory box along with the little circle under the exclamation point.

It wasn't long until Jane had met Tom. I guess it was inevitable. Hayden, after all, was our Everyman, the ultimate achievement for someone climbing the ladder of moral superiority. He had begun SDS. He had gotten beat up during Mississippi Summer. He had been involved in the urban insurrection in Newark. He had gone to Hanoi. When Tom came to Berkeley in 1968, his move was a validation of the city's status as a radical state of mind. (That was in the last stage of this once great city's fall from grace, before a jaded graffiti artist could capture its essence by scrawling this sentence on a one of the few remaining virgin walls — "Berkeley: too small to be a nation state, too large to be an insane asylum"). We were buoyed by Tom's presence. It was like, "Oh, good, Tom's here. Now the Long March can begin."

Tom had the idea that Berkeley would be the first of a series of "liberated zones" which would eventually link up to overthrow Pig Amerika. When the Peoples' Park riots broke out in 1969, it seemed like our time, as Jesse Jackson says, had come. Tom was up in an attic writing what he called the Berkeley Liberation Manifesto, the most memorable plank of which defended the "right" of the people to "use hard drugs." Tom was convinced that Peoples' Park was the beginning of the end for Pig Amerika. He had called the Black Panthers "our Vietcong" and was anxious to see them begin the civil war. David Hilliard was just then the Panthers' maximum leader because Huey was in jail, Cleaver had fled to Algeria, and Bobby Seale was under indictment for the death of Alex Rackley. Tom proposed to Hilliard that the Panthers maximize the contradictions by shooting down one of the Alameda

County Sheriff's helicopters. In one of the great comments of the Sixties, Hilliard gave him a heavy look and replied, "Just like you, Tom. Get a nigger to pull the trigger."

Peoples' Park was not the spark that lit the Revolution, but Tom remained a hero until he finally left Berkeley in the early Seventies. He had been living in a collective called the Red Family. This was sort of a phi beta kappa of Left-wing communes. Those of us who hadn't been asked to pledge heard of them doing target practice in the foothills, having struggle sessions over whether or not it was bourgeois privatism to close the door when you used the bathroom. We heard that in their political education classes Tom had made North Korea a model for revolutionary fervor. Imagine, not just the Confucian Communism of Hanoi, but of Pyongyang too! Nothing else shows quite so dramatically why Tom was a leader and the rest of us were followers.

But he finally got purged from the Red Family. It was the women who were his undoing. He was, they charged, insensitive and calculating in his relationships, too male-identified. But Tom apparently had unplumbed depths. Just a few weeks ago I interviewed an ex-Red Family female who told me that Tom had often worn cowboy boots when he had sex with the oppressed women of the commune. Cowboy boots and sex: no wonder Hilton Kramer hates the New Left.

Expelled from the Red Family, Tom landed on his feet, or with his boots on, if you will, when he linked up with Jane. It was a match made in heaven: her looks and his Leninism. (The reverse, of course, would have been a disaster). Not a Leninism of the book, perhaps, but certainly a Leninism of the soul. She went to North Vietnam and did her Hanoi Jane act. He formed the Indochina Peace Campaign after she returned and together they made sure, even after all the American troops were gone, that Congress cut off funds to the South Vietnamese government. After Hanoi had triumphed and spread night and fog throughout Southeast Asia, Joan Baez and some of the rest of us tried to protest, and Tom and Jane came down on us like a ton of bricks for betraying the Vietnamese revolution.

But of course it was in Hollywood, to bring this shaggy dog story back to its source, that Tom and Jane had their apotheosis. Jane had said periodically that she wanted to quit films and become a full-time activist. But she went back to Hollywood and Hollywood, in the next few years, came back to her. And now, Hollywood, thanks to Jane, is one of the last places where it is possible to be a full-time activist.

Jane's great insight was that people exhausted by role playing as a profession, actors, desperately wanted authenticity and that radical politics could give it to them. It had worked for her, after all. The film community was a lumpen for her and Tom when they became the Mork and Mindy of California politics. They not only brought the disparate Leftists together into a united front, but began to organize a new generation, the so-called Brat Pack, arranging things so that the torch of political wisdom could eventually be passed to figures like Ally Sheedy and Rob Lowe.

Something changed as a result of their efforts. There had always been trendy Lefties in Hollywood, people who would support Stalin and then cry Inquisition when McCarthy came looking for them. There had always been groupies who would come to Beverly Hills cocktail parties where people like Daniel Ortega and Reuben Zamorra were served up as the latest in radical *chic*. There had always been willing contributors to political campaigns, even people like Warren Beatty who got it into his head that he could make Gary Hart into a sort of Manchurian Candidate. But now every airhead starlet in Hollywood has politics. The careers of major stars are incomplete without a cause. Some like Barbara Streisand and Richard Dreyfuss have political advisors to help them chart the waters of the Left. They form *focos*, and get briefings and achieve, God save us, "empowerment," a term much in vogue among the members of the Holly-Left these days. And in their spare time, when they can take a moment from lobbying for the homeless and for the environment and for what is called in Hollywood "the choice issue," they make movies about Central America and other subjects.

It used to be that it required someone like Tom and Jane to make it happen, but thanks to them this situation is now self-propelling and can survive their split. It is a modern version of the Dunciad, which as those of you who have passed your cultural literacy tests will know, is Alexander Pope's mock epic about the pervasive triumph of dullness in every aspect of human experience. Except that instead of dullness it is Leftism that is spreading in Hollywood.

Where to end all this? Speaking to this particular group, devoted to the minutiae of the Hiss-Chambers case, I hope it will not seem pandering on my part if I say that it puts me in mind of Whittaker Chambers. I'm not referring to that part of Chambers involved with Hiss. I met Alger in the mid-Seventies, by the way. My publisher wanted me to write an anti-Allen Weinstein book[§] and arranged a lunch that led to other meetings. Even though I was still a demi-Leftist then and didn't doubt Hiss' innocence, I couldn't stand the guy. I guess it was partly the name — Hiss: I felt that he had a reptilian quality, eyes that held you like prey and skin that looked cold to the touch. And talking to him was like playing tennis against a wall — the ball came back just as hard as you hit it and no harder.

When I say that this all puts me in mind of Chambers, therefore, it has nothing to do with what he himself called "the great case." It has to do with his moving credo in *Witness* about knowing that he has traded the winning world for the losing world. Today the Communist Movement which obsessed Chambers is dead or dying, although we still see its slime trail all around us. Yet if he were alive now, I think that he would still feel that same heroic melancholy and isolation that he did a generation ago. Moreover, he would probably feel that *they* were still winning. And he would certainly see the savage irony in the fact that *they* were no longer the Commissars and Secret Agents of the Kremlin, but university professors deconstructing America and movie stars forcing political correctness. Standing here on Halloween night, the night of the Pumpkin Papers which were so much a part of Chambers' myth, one can imagine his reaction to the fact that the final offensive against Western values should be led not by Stalin and Molotov but by Ed Asner and Morgan Fairchild. What a savage smile this would cause on that snaggle-toothed mouth! What a look on that Jack O'Lantern face! □

[§] Weinstein's book *Perjury* established Hiss' guilt in the case.

Chapter Six

Carl Bernstein's Communist Problem
and Mine

by David Horowitz

More than a decade ago, when I was already in my late thirties and living in California, I was visited by an elderly woman whom I shall call Emily, the mother of my best childhood friend. Like my own parents and indeed all the adults I knew in the years when I was growing up, Emily had been a member of the Communist Party. She had come to discuss an incident that occurred when she was in the Party, and that still troubled her now nearly twenty years later. Although I still considered myself part of the Left at that time, I had already developed some publicly expressed doubts about the radical heritage we all had shared, and it was for this reason that Emily now sought me out: to confess her complicity in a crime committed when she was a Communist long ago.

Emily and my parents belonged to a colony of Jewish Communists who in the early Forties had settled in a ten-block neighborhood of working class Catholics in Sunnyside, Queens. The members of this colony lived two lives. Outwardly they were middle class: scrupulous in their respect for the mores of the community and unfailing in their obedience to its civil laws. They always identified themselves publicly as political "progressives," espousing views that were superficially liberal and democratic. They thought of themselves (and were perceived by others) as "socially conscious" and "idealistic" and were active in trade unions and civil rights groups and in the "progressive wing" of the Democratic Party.

The picture is consistent with that myth now struggling to be born in our literary culture, that these people were small "c" communists,

A slightly different version of this article appeared in Commentary, *July 1989.*

whose belief in democratic values far outweighed their commitment to big "C" Communism. But this is a mendacious myth, as well as malevolent in its revisionism. In fact, the members of this colony like Emily and my parents also inhabited another, secret world as soldiers in the Third International founded by Lenin. In their eyes a sixth of humanity had entered an entirely new stage of history in Soviet Russia in 1917, a triumphant humanity that would be extended all over the world by the actions of the loyal Communist vanguard which they had joined. The world of liberal and progressive politics may have been the world in which outsiders saw them, but their secret membership in this revolutionary army was the world that really mattered to Emily and my parents and to all their political friends. It was the world that gave real significance and meaning to what otherwise were modest and rather ordinary lives.

In their own minds Emily and my parents were secret agents. When they joined the Communist Party, they had even been given secret names for the time when their true objective would require them to abandon the facade of their liberal politics and go "underground" to take the lead in the revolutionary struggle. (My mother's secret name was "Anne Powers," which always struck me as terribly WASP.) All their legitimate political activities were merely preparations or fronts for the real tasks of their political commitment which they could discuss only with other secret agents like themselves. Their activities in the democratic organizations they entered and controlled, and in the liberal campaigns they promoted were all part of their secret service. Their real purpose in pursuing them was not to advance liberal or democratic values but to serve the interests of the Soviet state: because in their minds the Soviet Union was the place where the future had already begun.

For those in the Party, the revolutionary role was not the fantasy it seems in retrospect — a kitsch fantasy at that — but something that was very real indeed. The story that Emily told me proves this once again. No more than five feet tall in her stocking feet, Emily had been a high school teacher of foreign languages. Her only flirtation with a reality beyond the prudent bounds of her middle class existence was, in fact, her membership in the Communist Party. But even her Party life — despite its little Bolshevik rituals and conspiratorial overtones — was organized around activities that were quite unextraordinary: raising funds for the Spanish volunteers, marching for civil rights, and playing the part of a loyal cadre in the New York City Teacher's Union, which the Party controlled. But on one occasion Emily was chosen for a task that was not like the others, that would burden her with guilt for the rest of her life.

In 1940, the Party singled out Emily, then a new mother, for a special mission. The nature of the mission required that its purpose not be revealed, even to her, and that its details be concealed even from her Party comrades. In any other area of Emily's life, the intimations of illegality and danger inherent in such a proposal would have provoked intolerable anxieties and suspicions in a person of her middle class temperament and sheltered experience. But it was the Party that had made the request. And because it was the Party, the same elements had an opposite effect. The fear that was present only emphasized the portent of the Cause that beckoned. The prospect of danger only heightened the honor of receiving a call from the Party. She understood instinctively, now, that it was the very insignificance of her life, its unobtrusiveness, that made her suitable for the important task ahead. It was the Party that spoke, but it was History that called.

Emily agreed to undertake the Party's mission. She left her infant son with her husband in New York, and took a plane to Mexico. There she delivered a sealed envelope to a contact the Party had designated. After making the delivery she flew back to New York and resumed the life she had lived before. It was as simple as that. Yet it was not so simple at all. As Emily soon discovered, she had become a small but decisive link in the chain by which Joseph Stalin reached out from Moscow to Cayocoan, Mexico, to put an ice pick in Leon Trotksy's head.

In retrospect, one of the most disturbing elements in Emily's story lay in the fact that she had waited so long to tell it, and then only to me, privately. It had been twenty years after Khrushchev's Report about the crimes of Stalin, about the same time that she (and my parents) had left the Communist Party. She told her story to me now to relieve her guilt; but neither she nor my parents had ever thought to tell me this or similar stories to warn me of the minefields I might encounter, when as a young man I started on my own career in the Left. They never told their stories publicly, nor would they approve of me doing so now. The attitude of

Emily and my parents towards historical truth was a telling one. Like thousands of others, they had left the Party, but could not leave the faith.

Al Bernstein, the father of Watergate journalist Carl Bernstein, was a secret agent in the same way that Emily and my parents were secret agents and, like them, Al Bernstein is one of those progressives who left the Party but could never leave its political faith. When Carl Bernstein approached his father about the book he intended to write on "the witch-hunts leading up to the McCarthy era," Al Bernstein stonewalled him, refusing to be interviewed. He did not approve his son's quest for the truth about his Communist past. He did not want his son to discover the truth about his experience in the Communist Party, or about the Party's role in American life. He did not want him to write about it. To even ask the questions his son was asking, indicated that his political attitude was incorrect:

> I think your focus on the Party is cockeyed. You're up the wrong tree. The right tree is what people did....I worry about your premise. The *right* premise, the premise of a lot of recent books about the period, is that people were persecuted because of what they did, not because of their affiliation. Because once you admit affiliation you get into all that Stalinist crap.... (emphasis in original)

Not to accept the "right" premise was more than politically incorrect; it was dangerous:

> The premise people eventually accepted after the McCarthy period was that the victims weren't Communists. If you're going to write a book that says McCarthy was right, that a lot of us were Communists, you're going to write a dangerous book....You're going to prove McCarthy right, because all he was saying was that the system was loaded with Communists. And he was right.

In Al Bernstein's view, even though McCarthy was right about the presence of Communists posing as liberals in the political woodwork, and even though virtually all of McCarthy's victims were Communists, the fact that they were Communists (and lied about being Communists) had nothing to do with their being singled out:

> Was I 'oppressed' because I was a Communist?... No. It was incidental. I
> was 'oppressed' because of what I did, because I was affiliated with a
> left-wing union.

We should not be misled by the fatuousness of this catechism. The
sacrament the father rams down the throat of the son is brutal as well
as tasteless. In point of fact, Al Bernstein *was* a Communist; he was not
merely "affiliated with" the United Public Workers of America; he was
a leader of the union. The UPWA was not merely a "left-wing union,"
but a union under Communist Party control. And the fact that it was a
union under Communist control — despite Al Bernstein's protestations
— made it a different order of union entirely than other unions that
were not Communist controlled.

The difference was manifested most dramatically in the Cold War
year 1948, which began with the Communist coup in Czechoslovakia.
Coming twenty years after Munich, this event sent shock waves through
the capitals of the West. In an effort to halt the march of Soviet power,
the Truman Administration announced it was launching the Marshall
Plan — an economic aid program to revive the war-shattered economies
of Western Europe and to shore up its democracies against their own
Communist threats. While most American unions supported the Marshall Plan as an economic boon for their members and a necessary
defense measure for the West, Al Bernstein's union did not. Along with
all the other Communist-controlled unions in America, Al Bernstein's
United Public Workers attacked the Marshall Plan as a "Cold War" plot,
and launched an all-out campaign against it. On the political front, Al
Bernstein and his comrades bolted the Democratic Party and organized
the Progressive Party candidacy of Henry Wallace in the hope of
unseating Truman and ending his anti-Communist program.

It was because of the Communist campaign to support the Soviet
offensive in Eastern Europe that Al Bernstein's union (and other Communist-controlled unions) were purged from the CIO — not by
McCarthy or by Harry Truman and his Loyalty Board, but by unionists
like Philip Murray and Walter Reuther, who were liberal socialists and
who condemned the Stalinists for betraying their union members to the
interests of the Soviet Union. Phillip Murray, who is cited in passing in
Carl Bernstein's *Loyalties* for his principled opposition to the Loyalty

Boards, also told the CIO convention in 1948 that he opposed the Communists "because they have subverted every decent movement into which they have infiltrated themselves in the course of their unholy career."

At seventy-plus years of age, more than three decades after Senator McCarthy's death, Al Bernstein is still actively practicing his old Stalinist deceits, still taking the Fifth amendment towards any inquiry, however innocent, into his commitments and beliefs, still hiding his Communist agendas behind a liberal facade. And not only to the world at large, but to his own pathetically inquisitive son. To be called a witch-hunter by your father, while only trying, however ineffectually, to sort out the Oedipal tangle must be a daunting experience.

Carl, whose memoir is utterly innocent of the vast literature on American Communism (which refutes virtually every page of the book he has taken eleven years to write), measures the dimensions of his filial love in a passage that occurs a little less than halfway through the text: "Many years later,.....[I] realized that it is my father for whom I write, whose judgment I most respect, whose approval I still seek." *Loyalties* is little more than a unilateral withdrawal from the Oedipal struggle.

In the end it is the sheer desperation of this filial hunger which overwhelms the text Carl Bernstein intended to write and which explains the deficiencies of the preposterous book he has had the bad judgment to publish as *Loyalties* (even the title — originally *Disloyal* — has been changed to fit the fashions of the paternal Party line). He resists his father's "correct premise," manfully at the outset, but by the final chapters of *Loyalties* he has capitulated and even joined up. Al Bernstein's Communist Party loyalties didn't matter (either to him or to those who pursued him), Carl avows. He and all the other agents of the Communist cause were targeted solely for their activities on behalf of trade unionism and civil rights, and the internal security program of the Truman Administration "really was a war against liberals."

This is not a book about the Communist Party and its discontents, but a lecture on the need to keep the tattered faith at whatever cost to one's integrity. Rapidly expiring all over the world, this faith, strange to say, is alive and well in literary America. As Al Bernstein — the possessor of a shrewder, stronger intellect than his wayward son — impatiently observes, "the *right* premise" — the Communist Party's premise — is "the premise of a lot of recent books about the period." Thus, the standard academic work on the subject of American universities in the loyalty oath era — *No Ivory Tower* by Princeton Professor Eleanor Schrecker — is written from this neo-Stalinist perspective. As are most other recent studies, written by academic Leftists, about the early Cold War security conflicts.

Even more striking support for Al Bernstein's observation is offered by the notices of *Loyalties* in the most prestigious book reviews — The Sunday New York and LA *Times* and the Washington *Post*. In each, Carl had his literary knuckles rapped by Leftist reviewers who chided him for not justifying his parents' Communist politics *enough*. Thus, Paul Robeson's neo-Stalinist biographer Professor Martin Duberman complained in the "Book World" of the Washington *Post*:

> In his dedication, Carl Bernstein asserts that he is 'proud of the choices' his parents made. But he never provides enough argued detail about what went into those choices to allow most Americans to join him — as surely they should—in his approbation.

What are the tenets of the neo-Stalinist faith that has so unexpectedly resurfaced in American letters? Basically there are two. The first — that Communists were peace-loving, do-gooding, civil rights activists and American patriots; the second — that they were the innocent victims of a fascist America. Carl has it down pat:

> *'It was a reign of terror.'*
> I have never heard my father talk like that, have never known him to reach for a cliche. But this was no cliche. (emphasis in original)

No, it was not a cliche; it is a lie. No, Carl, we didn't have a reign of terror — at least not in the way that phrase is understood to apply to the Stalinist world out of which our families both came and where it means blood in the gutters. My mother, for example, elected to take an early "disability" retirement from the New York school system rather than answer questions about her membership in the Party. But with the help of Party friends and liberal sympathizers she immediately went on to other more lucrative careers. Your father became a small-time entrepreneur and you got a job (through his personal connections) as a reporter at the Washington *Star*. When, later, you were at the *Post* and about to help topple a sitting President, you went to Managing Editor Ben Bradlee to reveal the terrible secret about your parents' Communist past, and what did he do? Remove you from the case? No, in horrific, anti-Communist, paranoid America, America home of the reign of terror, the editor of the Washington *Post* told you to get on with the story. And what did you learn from that? Exactly nothing.

And that is my final complaint about *Loyalties* and its pseudo account of the anti-Communist era. As in all the other recent rewrites of this history, whose premise is to keep the faith, the reality of the post-war domestic conflict between Communists and anti-Communists is simply unreported. In a fleeting episode in *Loyalties,* for example, Carl's friend and former boss Ben Bradlee recalls over dinner that he had always thought of progressives like Carl's parents (whom personally he did not know) as "awful people." Even in the jagged structure of this book, the observation is jarring, but far more jarring is the fact that the famous investigative reporter of Watergate does not pursue the remark to inquire what memories might lie behind it. The same lack of inquisitiveness is seen in his feeble efforts to understand the nature of his parents' true commitments. He describes his mother, then in her seventies, for example, as a woman who is "very forgiving." But when she refers to a political adversary of thirty years ago as a "vicious bastard," her son simply ignores the emotional signal, thus missing anything that it might tell us about the polarized psyches of political progressives like his parents.

Elsewhere, he describes how his grandfather would take him to a Jewish bookstore to buy the Yiddish-language Communist newspaper *Freiheit.* "Until the day he died in 1967 he had no use for the [non-Communist] *Forward* — or the [non-Communist] Socialists. '*Fareters,*' traitors of the cause, he called them, and he didn't much like having any of them into his house..." This life-long hatred towards non-Communist Leftists, coupled with casual vitriolic abuse, was a staple of the progressive personalities of Carl Bernstein's parents and of the other "victims" of the postwar "purge." In attempting to explain to Carl, at another point in the text, why Al Bernstein joined the Party, family friend Bob Treuhaft observed: "There was a feeling that unless you joined and were with us you were the enemy." Carl lets this one slip by too.

There were many enemies. John L. Lewis, head of the CIO's United Mine Workers, was once a Party ally, but when he refused to go along with the Communist-supported no-strike pledge after the German invasion of Russia, the Party attacked him as a "pro-Nazi" who was committing "treason." The Communists also routinely denounced civil rights leader A. Philip Randolph, the organizer of the wartime March on Washington, as "a fascist helping defeatism," because Randolph refused to shelve the struggle for civil rights — as the Party dictated — in favor of joining the effort to help save the USSR from defeat. So much for the fantasy that Communist Party members were at bottom only unionists and civil rights activists.

Not only were they not libertarians, they were also, despite their pious wails later on, notorious masters of the political blacklist in all the organizations they managed to control. It was partly for these reasons, that when the Loyalty Boards and the Congressional Committees finally did come to town, there were a lot of people — a lot of liberal people — waiting to settle scores with the Communists. To them, Communists were not the civil libertarian idealists of Carl Bernstein's book, but political conspirators who had infiltrated and manipulated and taken over their own liberal organizations, and subverted them for hidden agendas; who had slandered, libeled and blacklisted them when they had opposed the Party line; who had *lied* to the public, pretending that they were not Marxists or loyal to Soviet Russia when questions about their political affiliations were asked.

The Communists lied to everyone then, and the new keepers of their faith are still lying today. "If you're going to write a book that says McCarthy was right, that a lot of us were Communists, you're going to write a dangerous book," Al Bernstein warned. Look at the logic here: to admit that they were Communists is to lend credence to the claims of Joseph McCarthy. Why is this dangerous at this late date? Is not McCarthy himself the most irretrievable political corpse of the McCarthy era? It is dangerous not because it will bring persecution, but because it will penetrate the final veil that allows a life to appear to be something more than simple service in the ranks of totalitarianism.

It is not fear of libeling an "innocent" association that haunts the political Left; it is something more like the fear that haunted the conscience of deconstructionist scholar Paul De Man: embarrassment over a guilt that was real:

> 'Look,' [Al Bernstein] snapped, 'you've read Lillian Hellman's book. She skirts these questions [about Communist Party membership] very neatly. She's too sharp to leave herself open to that kind of embarrassment.'

As always, Al Bernstein's old Stalinist politics reveal a sharper judgment than that of his born-again son. *Embarrassment* is the problem — not a sham reign of terror; it is the shame of possible exposure as having been a loyal supporter of a mass murderer like Stalin for all those years.

The struggle now is not over the fact, but what it *meant* to be a Communist. Civil rights, trade unionism, human brotherhood and peace: that's what we were — they now stubbornly claim as their final fall-back position — that was our cause. Communism? Marxism? Socialism? Those were incidental — irrelevant to who we were and what we did.

Loyalties reveals the secret of how the Left aims to be born again — by erasing the embarrassment of its disreputable past; by hiding the shame of having supported Stalin and Mao and Fidel and Ho, and all the terrible purges, murders and other despicable means which finally served no beneficial ends. The ultimate embarrassment is of having been so stubbornly and perversely on the wrong side of history; of having embraced "solutions" that were morally and politically and economically bankrupt in the great struggles of our time. As Joseph Stalin was the first socialist to truly understand, the airbrushing of history is the only sure means to preserve the honor of the Left. In this, as no doubt in other things in his undiscovered life, Al Bernstein follows right along the Stalinist path. And his son walks in lockstep behind him, picking up his mess. ☐

Chapter Seven

Keepers of the Flame

(Peter Collier & David Horowitz)

The Church of Radicalism administers a harsh communion and has no patience with apostates. We knew this before and discovered it again when we published *Destructive Generation*. The book is not a plea for grace, but an attempt to understand the varieties of religious experience that characterized the Movement in its heyday and among its hardcore; to understand what went wrong with the Sixties Left, what responsibility people like ourselves bear, and how the faith of Leftism has been kept going in our own time despite an unrelieved record of disaster.

In writing *Destructive Generation*, of course, we expected to be excommunicated from the Church of the Left yet again. But this time, in addition to being shown the exit sign at the gates of Eden, we found ourselves stigmatized as something even worse than anti-Left. We were *anti-Sixties*! In writing about the decade, we had stumbled into the nostalgia factory where the touch-up artists of radical history work with airbrushes to erase unpleasant memories and smooth out rough moments. We had seen the smithy where the myths of this golden age are forged; myths intended to restore the power of the radical dream and to make sure that our present political culture doesn't learn from its history so that it will be condemned to repeat it.

Of these myths about the Sixties, the first and most pernicious is the doctrine of original innocence. This holds that the Left is purer of heart and therefore better — more compassionate, idealistic, peace-loving and humane — than all other political beliefs. To re-manufacture this innocence, defenders of Sixties radicalism must now propose that

---

This chapter appeared June 26, 1989 in The New Republic *in response to radical critics of* Destructive Generation. *It has been slightly edited for this volume.*

groups such as the Black Panther Party and the Weatherman terrorists — groups of which we had enough first-hand knowledge to write about them plausibly in *Destructive Generation* — were nothing more than a lunatic fringe that had only miniscule support 20 years ago and have no legitimate standing as historical metaphors today. There might have been excesses back then — justifications of "revolutionary violence," a fashion for zany neo-Marxist creeds. But those involved in such things were part of what university administrators once called "a small but vociferous minority" — a minority which gets smaller with each passing year as yesterday's Leftists pop out of their cocoons and take wing as today's progressives.

"It wasn't us, babe," these fluttering revisionists say today. *We* were not violent. *You* might have been, but not us. *We* were not proponents of revolution or even radical change. Of course, somebody did it. Since *you* admit in your book that these things took place, *you* are guilty. Such is the fate of those who use the second person plural as part of the grammar of collective responsibility.

For us, there is an irony in being called the last New Left extremists. Having actually drawn back from the Sixties Left during its heaviest weather, we thought that when *Destructive Generation* appeared we might be criticized by remnants of the hardcore as being inauthentic. Where were you when we were getting ready for the armed revolution? we imagined them asking. But we obviously misjudged the strength of the historical rewrite now under way. Our old comrades have pointed the finger instead of clenching the fist. "You guys were part of the lunatic fringe then and you're part of it now," they have said of us. "You've just exchanged one radicalism for another while the rest of us have been integrating ourselves back into society and getting on with our lives." Or, as *New Republic* editor Hendrik Hertzberg complained to us in a recent conversation, "You were apologists for communism then and you are apologists for anti-communism now." (As though these postures were morally equivalent).

Tom Hayden, Bobby Seale, and all the other quick change artists of the Left have a right to get on with their lives. But they have no right to deface the truth of the Sixties to ease their mid-life transits. Yet one looks in vain in Hayden's autobiography *Renuion* for any serious admission of complicity in the North Vietnamese rape of South Vietnam. Or for any illumination on the year or so he spent perpetually out of breath from trying to inflate the revolutionary legend of the Black Panthers as "America's Viet Cong." Or for any mention of his experiences in the hills of Northern California doing target practice under the tutelage of the Minister of Defense of the "Red Family" in giddy anticipation of the fascism he thought Richard Nixon might install, thus giving a little goose to the revolution which had then entered a period of dry labor.

Hayden was no worse than many at the time. But he is no better now because he has decided to subtract these facts from his own life and from the history of the Movement in the interests of getting on with it. This lack of second thoughts is the telltale heart of the American Left.

Why no reckoning? Because reckonings are conservative. They counsel against the heedless rush to try to redeem the ambiguous and mottled realities of the human condition. They prove that life is made better only incrementally and with great difficulty, but it is made worse — much worse — very easily. Reckonings examine the toxic waste revolutionary enthusiasms leave in their wake. Reckonings open the mass graves to examine the shards of bone which are all that is left of the New Men and Women created by utopias past.

Because they want to continue their crusades, our old comrades not only don't want second thoughts of their own, but they don't want us to have them either. They not only want to protect their sense of moral superiority as a special generation formed by a crucial decade, but also keep that decade inviolate so that some future radical generation can use it as a model when it decides to pull the sword from the stone.

A second myth of Sixties nostalgia artists is that "we" were actually more sinned against than sinning. In fact, "we" never really "knew sin" at all (to use Todd Gitlin's phrase in *The Sixties*) until the end of the decade when the unending war had blunted our moral affect and driven us into a state of temporary insanity.

In the battle between memory and forgetting, this is an example not only of amnesia but of auto-lobotomy. The New Left bit the apple the first time the first journalist thrust the first microphone into its face and told it that it was a prophetic minority. It knew sin early in the Sixties in the founding sessions of SDS when Hayden and others tried to propose a moral equivalence between the U.S. and the U.S.S.R.; in the middle of the decade when it claimed that Ho Chi Minh was the George Washington of his country; and at the end of the decade when it transmuted the slogan "Bring the troops home" into "Bring the war home."

To serve memory means admitting that *we* (we radicals generically, not just we two) did not love this country enough. We did not do all we could to stop the war without hating our heritage root and branch. If we did not carry North Vietnamese flags ourselves, we did not face down those who did. If we did not spell Amerika with a "k" ourselves, we failed to repudiate those who did. There was enough sin to go around in the Sixties, sins of omission as well as commission, sins of the heart as well as the hand.

The fault lines concerning the Sixties and the Left in our culture go deep. Exactly how deep we realized when *Village Voice* Leftist Paul Berman, who had attacked us in print on several previous occasions as "renegades" (a term of the Thirties that has outlived the Stalinist neologicians who created it), was given our book by *The New Republic* for an unusually lengthy review. Because our position on issues such as the spread of totalitarianism in Central America were closer to the magazine's than those of Berman, who has vacillated between being a cheerleader for the Sandinistas and a fence-sitter in the struggle over Nicaragua's future, this assignment had the feel of a political hit.

A 1986 Berman article in *Mother Jones*, magazine of the long radical exile, opens with a scene in which the author is in Managua chumming it up with Omar Cabezas, the number two cop in Tomas Borge's Ministry of the Interior. It seems that he had just read Cabezas' autobiography *Fire From the Mountain* and was "astonished" — not by the fact that Cabezas had falsified the history of the revolution, but rather by the intoxicating discovery that "backwater Nicaragua was the world center of the New Left..." Proceeding from this *apercu*, Berman wrote: "Elsewhere, the dream of Che led to stupid posturings. [But] in Leon [where Cabezas launched his Sandinista career] the dream of Che was the road to the Ministry of the Interior. Fantasy elsewhere was realism in Nicaragua."

Here is the authentic voice of the Sixties Left thrown as if by ventriloquism into the present. Twenty years ago, we saw the Fidelistas as archetypal New Leftists, the ones who had *done it* while we pampered Americans were only fantasizing about it. Cuba having proved unpalatable, it is now the Sandinistas who have the authenticity America's radicals never achieved. There is no acknowledgement that in Cuba, Che's New Left dream led directly to Fidel's gulag. Here it might be different, Berman muses, while sitting in the headquarters of the Sandinista police state batting his eyes at another dreamer of Che's dream.

Berman typifies those intellectuals of the Left who always wind up — for all their birdwalking and backtracking — on the wrong side. Determined to locate the *good* part of the New Left in this newest workers' paradise, he dons his Mexican wedding shirt and *huarches* and wanders through Managua in pinched face concentration searching for evidence that socialism cares about people. We saw him there in the fall of 1987 and were amused by the mumbled apologies he made for having the *betisse* to stay a couple of nights in the Intercontinental Hotel and by the quick dash he made every morning to breathe the heady fumes of the *barrio*.

It is not surprising that the whole literary repertory of Leftism is on display in his attack on our book — the shameless mendacity, the fabulation of history, the brain-dwarfing moral smugness, and above all the insuperable intellectual mediocrity. Berman is not only ignorant about basic realities of the decade we write about, he is also tone deaf to the era's complexity. This is shown by what he writes about the Black Panthers. Collier and Horowitz alone, he fatuously suggests, got an illicit thrill from these heavy dudes; only we were intrigued by their Promethean willingness to pick up the gun; only we suspended our disbelief when they said they had put the gun down in favor of serving the people.

The Panthers were, in fact, an icon for the great mass of worshipers in the Church of Leftism, a larger and more joyous congregation then than now. The posters of Huey P. Newton sitting on his Zulu throne adorned the walls of hip lawyers as well as college students. Leonard Bernstein didn't invite just anyone into his living room even in those balmy days. Berman has the gall to ignore it all. Aint nobody here but us moderates, he says; we didn't believe in no Black Panthers back then.

The irony is that it was only *after* the "violent" faction (which followed Eldridge Cleaver) was expelled from the Party in the early Seventies that people such as ourselves, who had actually remained aloof from the Panthers during their maximalist phase, did get involved. And, as we point out in *Destructive Generation*, we did so because Huey Newton claimed not only to have put down the gun but to have embraced exactly the sort of community organizing and development passionately believed in by that tiny group of social democrats among whom Berman now counts himself. Like Berman and his ilk today, we wanted back then to continue to believe in the Left. We were searching for a soulful socialism in the Oakland ghetto just as he now searches for it in the *barrio* of Managua. Of course we were wrong fifteen years ago just as he is today. The "sane" wing of the Black Panther Party turned out to be filled with insane killers.

But if we were wrong, we were far from alone in our self-delusion, as Berman claims. About the time we became involved in the Panthers' "survival" programs, Bobby Seale came surprisingly close to being elected Mayor of Oakland. In the spring of 1973, the *Nation* ran a long article explaining the change for the better that had taken place in the Party. Rutgers political scientist Ross Baker assured readers that it was safe to support the Panthers once again because they had "outgrown their rhetoric."

A few months *after* the two of us became involved with the Panthers, Murray Kempton wrote a front page review of Newton's *Revolutionary Suicide* in the New York *Times Book Review* which concludes with this peroration: "...We must hear him out because we suspect that he comes not as avenger but as healer. Here is the only visible American who has managed to arrive at the Platonic conception of himself..." In a final flourish Kempton noted that Huey had run a joint seminar at Yale with Erik Erikson, using the reference to compare the Panther leader favorably to Luther and Gandhi. That was in May 1973. A few weeks later, *The Briar Patch*, Kempton's own book on the "Panther 21," was published.

And it was favorably reviewed by another *soi disant* social democrat, Garry Wills, who served up another front page *Times* review containing such gems about the Panthers — the Eldridge Cleaver Panthers, no less — as these: "Never, it would seem, have people threatened more and been guilty of less.... And in the end there is a sense of the almost incredible ability of men to find dignity in resisting the viciousness of other men — like lifting a 500-pound weight with one hand while stooped under a 1,000-pound weight kept on one's back."

The image is as awkward as many of Berman's own, but the message is clear: these noble Panthers were victims. Thus Kempton and Wills said in the liberal *New York Times* what even we, at this stage, would have thought a bit much. So, our sin is not in being the only ones who enthused over the Black Panthers in 1973, but being the only ones who care to remember today the nasty things that took place back then when Huey Newton was still a fetish object for liberals and social democrats, as well as scraggly West Coast radicals.

The story we tell of the Panther *gotterdamerung*, moreover, would remain trapped in the memory hole of the Left if not for *Destructive Generation*. We alone have pointed out what Berman claims is obvious: that the Panthers, for all their success in blandishing liberals and social democrats, had *never* been anything more than a violent street gang. Protective of the faith, Berman bristles when we apply this term to the hardcore Left as a whole. Lest we forget, however, Bonnie and Clyde ("We rob banks") were as much cult heroes in the Sixties as Huey and Eldridge were. More prototypically, Stalin had a gang that also robbed banks. SDS wound up, after elemental mitosis, as a gang of terrorists called Weatherman. The Sandinstas are a gang in power; the FMLN is a gang, thus far anyhow, out of power; Castro is the last great revolutionary gangster in the Soviet world.

The metaphor may not be perfect, but it is apt because the gang, like the Left, is ruled by power, not laws; the gang aims only to perpetuate itself; the gang uses rackets and scams to accumulate its wealth (shaking down the Oakland ghetto, or shaking down the *campesinos*). The gang thrives on feudalism and backwardness; and as that darkness is lifted, as we see today in the Soviet bloc, the gang's hold is threatened. Of course, criminal gangs are often candid about themselves in a way that the gangs of the Left never are. Criminal gangs never say they are serving the people, for instance, or midwifing the birth of a socialist utopia.

Looking for love in all the wrong places, Berman is one of those socialist butterflies for whom the bloody and bankrupt history of socialism has no conclusive meaning. This is why he continues to travel to Managua and bring back reports that careen between agonizing reappraisal and reaffirmation of belief.

At home Berman postures as an independent, if sympathetic, critic of the revolution. In Managua, however, the desire to be a communicant in the Church of Socialism gets the better of him. He goes to see Cabezas and reports back that the Sandinistas are the only New Leftists who actually made it happen. The image of someone who postures as a Leftist of conscience sitting in the headquarters of the secret police has a cognitive dissonance right out of the Sixties. ◻

II

Liberation Fronts

Chapter One

My Vietnam Lessons

(David Horowitz)

When I see today's protesters, in the flush of youthful idealism, with their signs proclaiming "No Vietnams in Central America," a feeling of ineffable sadness overtakes me. For twenty years ago I was one of them. In 1962, as a graduate student at Berkeley I wrote the first book of New Left protest, *Student*, and helped to organize perhaps the first anti-war demonstration opposing what we denounced as U.S. intervention in Vietnam. In the mid-Sixties I went to England and helped to organize the Vietnam Solidarity Campaign, which supported what we called the Vietnamese struggle for independence from the United States, as well as the International War Crimes Tribunal which brought American war atrocities under intense and damning scrutiny but ignored atrocities committed by the Communist forces in Vietnam. While in England, I also wrote *The Free World Colossus*, a New Left history of the Cold War, which was used as a radical text in colleges and in the growing movement against the Vietnam War. At the end of the Sixties I returned to America as an editor of *Ramparts*, the most widely read New Left magazine. Our most famous cover appeared during Richard Nixon's campaign in 1972 for a second term. It featured a photograph of the My Lai massacre with a sign superimposed and planted among the corpses saying "Re-Elect the President."

Let me make this perfectly clear: Those of us, who inspired and then led the anti-war movement did not want just to stop the killing as so many veterans of those domestic battles now claim. We wanted the Communists to win. It is true that some of us may have said we only wanted the United States to get out of Vietnam, but we understood that

Speech to a Congressional seminar on the 10th anniversary of the fall of Saigon, April 10, 1985.

this meant the Communists would win. "Bring the troops home" was our slogan, the fall of Saigon was the result.

There was a political force in American life that did want a peace that would not also mean a Communist victory — a peace that would deny Hanoi its conquest and preserve the integrity of South Vietnam. That force was led by our arch-enemy President Richard Nixon, whose campaign slogans were "Peace with Honor" in Vietnam and "Law and Order" at home. Just as we did not want honor that meant preserving the government of South Vietnam, so we did not respect law and order, because respecting the democratic process would have meant that the majority in America, who supported President Nixon and South Vietnam, would have prevailed.

*   *   *

Like today's young radicals, we Sixties activists had a double standard when it came to making moral and political judgements. We judged other countries and political movements — specifically socialist countries and revolutionary movements — by the futures we imagined they could have if only the United States and its allies would get out of their way. We judged America, however, by its actual performance, which we held up to a standard of high and even impossible ideals. Of course, if we had looked at the facts (or been able to) we would have seen that America was more tolerant, more democratic and more open to change than the countries and movements to whom we gave our support. But we were unable to do just that. We were, in the then fashionable term, "alienated" from what was near to us, unable to judge it with any objectivity.

Some of this alienation — a perennial and essential ingredient of all political Leftism — could be attributed to youth itself, the feeling that we could understand the world better and accomplish more than our elders could. There was another dimension to our disaffection, however, an ideology that committed us to "truths" behind the common sense surfaces of things.

I, myself, was a Marxist and a socialist. I believed in the "dialectic" of history and, therefore, even though I knew that the societies calling themselves Marxist were ruled by ruthless dictatorships, I believed that they would soon evolve into socialist democracies. I attributed their negative features to under-development and to the capitalist pasts from which they had emerged. I believed that Marxist economic planning was the most rational solution to their under-development and would soon bring them unparalleled prosperity — an idea refuted as dramatically by the experience of the last seventy years as the ancillary notion that private property is the source of all tyranny and that socialist states would soon become free. (They might become free, but only by giving up their socialist delusions).

On the other hand, the same Marxist analysis told me that America, however amenable to reform in the past, was set on a course that would make it increasingly rigid, repressive, and ultimately fascist. The United States was the leviathan of a global imperialist system under attack at home and abroad. Its ruling class could not afford to retreat from this challenge; it could only grow more reactionary and repressive. This expectation, wrong in every respect, was not an idiosyncratic theory of mine, but was the lynchpin of the New Left's political view of the world generally and of its strategy of opposition to America's war in Vietnam in particular. The New Left believed that, in Vietnam, America's corporate liberal empire had reached a point of no return. As a result, electoral politics and any effort to reform it were futile and counter-productive. The only way to alter America's imperial course was to take to the streets — first to organize resistance to the war, and then to "liberate" ourselves from the corporate capitalist system. That was why we were in the streets. That was why we did not take a hard stand against the bomb throwers in our midst.

What happened to change my views and give me second thoughts? As our opposition to the war grew more violent and our prophecies of impending fascism more intense, I had taken note of how we were actually being treated by the System we condemned. By the decade's end we had (deliberately) crossed the line of legitimate dissent and abused every First Amendment privilege and right granted us as Americans. While American boys were dying overseas, we spat on the flag, broke the law, denigrated and disrupted the institutions of government and education, gave comfort and aid (even revealing classified secrets) to the enemy. Some of us provided a protective propaganda shield for Hanoi's Communist regime while it tortured American fliers; others engaged in violent sabotage against the war effort. All the time I thought to myself: if we did this in any other country, the very least of our punishments would be long prison terms and the pariah status of traitors. In any of the *socialist* countries we supported — from Cuba to North Vietnam — we would spend most of our lives in jail and more probably be shot.

And what actually happened to us in repressive capitalist America? Here and there our wrists were slapped (some of us went to trial, some spent months in jail) but basically the country tolerated us. And listened to us. We began as a peripheral minority, but as the war dragged on without an end in sight, people joined us: first in thousands and then in tens of thousands, swelling our ranks until finally we reached what can only be called the conscience of the nation. America itself became troubled about its presence in Vietnam, about the justice and morality of the war it had gone there to fight. And because the nation became so troubled, it lost its will to continue the war, and withdrew.

Out the window went all those preconceptions we had had about the rigidity of American politics, about the controlled capitalist media (which in fact provided the data that fueled our attacks on the war) and about the ruling class lock on American foreign policy. That policy had shown itself in its most critical dimension responsive to the will of ordinary people, and to their sense of justice and morality. As a historian, I believe I am correct in my judgment that America's withdrawal from the battlefront in Vietnam because of domestic opposition is unique in human history: there is no other case on record of a major power retreating from a war in response to the moral opposition of its own citizenry.

If America's response to this test of fire gave me an entirely new understanding of American institutions and of the culture of democracy which informs and supports them, the aftermath of the U.S. retreat gave me a new appreciation of the Communist opponent. America not only withdrew its forces from Vietnam, as we on the Left said it could never do, but from Laos and Cambodia, and ultimately from its role as guardian of the international status quo. Far from increasing the freedom and well-being of Third World nations, as we in the Left had predicted, however, America's withdrawal resulted in an international power vacuum that was quickly filled by the armies of Russia, Cuba, and the mass murderers of the Khmer Rouge (not to mention the non-Communist but no less bloodthirsty fanatics of revolutionary Islam). All this bloodshed and misery was the direct result of America's post-Vietnam withdrawal, of the end of *Pax Americana*, which we had ardently desired and helped to bring about.

In Vietnam itself, the war's aftermath showed beyond any doubt the struggle there was not ultimately to achieve or prevent self-determination but — as various Presidents said and we denied — a Communist conquest of the South. Today, the National Liberation Front of South Vietnam, whose cause we supported, no longer exists. Its leaders are dead, in detention camps, under house arrest, in exile, powerless. America left Vietnam ten years ago; but today Hanoi's army is the fourth largest in the world and Vietnam has emerged as a Soviet satellite and imperialist aggressor in its own right, subverting the independence of Laos, invading and colonizing Cambodia.

These events confronted me with a supreme irony: the nation I had believed to be governed by corporate interests, a fountainhead of world reaction, was halted in mid-course by its conscience-stricken and morally aroused populace; the forces I had identified with progress, once freed from the grip of U.S. "imperialism," revealed themselves to be oppressive, unspeakably ruthless and predatory. I was left with this question: what true friend of the South Vietnamese, or the Cambodians, or the Ethiopians, or the people of Afghanistan, would not wish that *Pax Americana* were still in force?

There was yet another Vietnam lesson for me when I pondered the question put by Jeane Kirkpatrick to the still-active veterans of the New Left: "How can it be that persons so deeply committed to the liberation of South Vietnam and Cambodia from Generals Thieu and Lon Nol were so little affected by the enslavement that followed their liberation? Why was there so little anguish among the American accomplices who helped Pol Pot to power?" Indeed, why have such supposedly passionate advocates of Third World liberation not raised their voices in protest over the rape of Afghanistan or the Cuban-abetted catastrophe to Ethiopia?

Not only has the Left failed to make a cause of these Marxist atrocities, it has failed to consider the implications of what we now know about Hanoi's role in South Vietnam's "civil war." For North Vietnam's victors have boldly acknowledged that they had intruded even more regular troops into the South than was claimed by the Presidential White Paper which was used to justify America's original commitment of military forces — a White Paper which we Leftists scorned at the time as a fiction based on anti-Communist paranoia and deception. But today's Left is too busy denigrating Ronald Reagan's White Papers on Soviet and Cuban intervention in Central America to consider the implications of this past history to the present.

My experience has convinced me that historical ignorance and moral blindness are endemic to the American Left, necessary conditions of its existence. It does not value the bounty it actually has in this country, and in the effort to achieve a historically bankrupt fantasy — call it socialism, call it "liberation" — undermines the very privileges and rights it is the first to claim.

The lesson I learned from Vietnam was not a lesson in theory, but a lesson in practice. Observing this nation go through its worst historical hour from a vantage point on the other side of the barricade, I came to understand that democratic values are easily lost and historically only rarely achieved, that America is a precious gift, a unique presence in the world of nations. Because it is the strongest of the handful of democratic societies that mankind has managed to create, it is also a fortress that stands between the free nations of the world and the dark, totalitarian forces which threaten to engulf them.

My values have not changed, but my sense of what supports and makes them possible has. I no longer can join "anti-war" movements that seek to disarm the Western democracies in the face of the danger that confronts them. I support the current efforts of America's leadership to rebuild our dangerously weakened military defenses, and I endorse the conservative argument that America needs to be vigilant, strong and clear of purpose in its life and death struggle with its global totalitarian adversaries. As an ex-radical, I would only add that in this struggle Americans need to respect and encourage their own generosity — their tolerance for internal dissent and their willingness to come to the aid of people who are fighting for their freedom. □

Chapter Two

Semper Fidel

(David Horowitz)

Twenty-five years ago, as one of the founders of the New Left, I was an organizer of the first political demonstrations on this Berkeley campus — and indeed on any campus — to protest our government's anti-Communist policies in Cuba and Vietnam. Tonight I come before you as a man I used to tell myself I would never be: a supporter of President Reagan, a committed opponent of Communist rule in Nicaragua. I make no apologies for my present position. It was what I thought was the humanity of the Marxist *idea* that made me what I was then; it is the inhumanity of what I have seen to be the Marxist *reality* that has made me what I am now. If my former comrades who support the Sandinista cause were to pause for a moment and then plunge their busy political minds into the human legacies of their activist pasts, they would instantly drown in an ocean of blood.

The real issue before us is not whether it is morally right for the United States to arm the contras, or whether there are unpleasant men among them. The issue before us and before all people who cherish freedom is how to oppose a Soviet imperialism so vicious and so vast as to dwarf any previously known. An "ocean of blood" is no metaphor. As we speak here tonight, this empire — whose axis runs through Havana and now Managua — is killing hundreds of thousands of Ethiopians to consolidate a dictatorship whose policies against its black citizens make the South African government look civilized and humane.

There is another issue, especially important to me, which is the credibility and commitment of the American Left, whose attitudes to

---

Speech for a debate on Nicaragua, given at the University of California, Berkeley, April 4, 1986.

American power have gained a far-reaching influence since the end of the Vietnam War.

In his speech on Nicaragua, President Reagan rightly invoked the precedent of the Truman Doctrine, the first attempt to oppose Soviet expansion through revolutionary surrogates in Greece. The first protest of my radical life was against the Truman Doctrine in a May Day march in 1948, and I was with the Left defending revolutions in Russia and China, in Eastern Europe and Cuba, in Cambodia and Vietnam. Just as the Left defends the Sandinistas now. And I remember clearly the arguments and "facts" with which we made our case in forums like this, and what the other side said too — the presidents who came and went, and the anti-Communists on the Right, the William Buckleys and the Ronald Reagans. And in every case, without exception, time has proven the Left wrong — tragically and destructively wrong. Wrong in its views of the revolutionaries' intentions, and wrong about the facts of their revolutionary rule. And just as consistently the anti-Communists were proven right.

Just as the Left now dismisses the President's warnings about Soviet expansion, calling them anti-Communist paranoia, a threat to the peace and a mask for American imperialism, so we attacked President Truman as the aggressor then. Russia's control of Eastern Europe we said was only a defensive buffer, a temporary response to American power — first, because Russia had no nuclear weapons and then, because it lacked the missiles to deliver them.

Today, the Soviet Union is a nuclear superpower, missiles and all, but it has not given up an inch of the empire which it gained during the Second World War — not Eastern Europe, not the Baltic states which Hitler delivered to Stalin and whose nationhood Stalin erased and who are now all but forgotten, not even the Kurile islands which were once part of Japan.

Not only have the Soviets failed to relinquish their conquests in all these years — years of dramatic, total decolonization in the West — but their growing strength and the wounds of Vietnam (a scab liberals and Leftists have continued to pick) have encouraged them to reach for more. South Vietnam, Cambodia, Laos, Ethiopia, Yemen, Mozambique, and Angola are among the nations which have recently fallen into the Soviet orbit. To expand their territorial core — which their apologists still refer to as a "defensive perimeter" — Moscow has already slaughtered a million peasants in Afghanistan, an atrocity warmly endorsed by the Sandinista government. Its Minister of Defense, Humberto Ortega, describes the army of the conquerors — whose scorched earth policy has driven half the population of Afghanistan from its homes — as the "pillar of peace" in the world today. To any self-respecting socialist, praise for such barbarism would be an inconceivable outrage — as it was to the former Sandinista, now Contra, Eden Pastora. But praise for the barbarians is sincere tribute coming from the Sandinista rulers, since they see themselves as an integral part of the Soviet empire itself.

The struggle of man against power is the struggle of memory against forgetting. So wrote the Czech writer Milan Kundera, whose name and work no longer exist in his homeland. In all the Americas, Fidel Castro was the only head of state to cheer the Russian tanks as they rolled over the brave people of Prague. And cheering right along with Fidel were Carlos Fonseca, Tomas Borge, Humberto Ortega, and the other creators of the present Nicaraguan regime. One way to assess what has happened in Nicaragua is to realize that wherever Soviet tanks crush freedom in the future, there will now be two governments in the Americas supporting them all the way — Cuba, where Castro sells his young men as Soviet legionnaires for billions of dollars a year, and Nicaragua, whose time to provide Soviet conscripts for empire will come, if and when the American Left manages to cut the Contras adrift.

Memory against power: about its own crimes and for its own criminals, the Left has no memory at all, which is the only reason it can wave its finger at President Reagan and the anti-Communist Right.

In the eyes of the Left I grew up in, along with the Sandinista founders, Stalin's Russia was a socialist paradise, the model of the liberated future of all mankind. Literacy to the uneducated, power to the weak, justice to the forgotten — we praised Russia then, just as the Left praises the Sandinistas now. And just as they ignore warnings like Violetta Chamorro's — "With all my heart, I tell you it is worse here now than it was in the times of the Somoza dictatorship" — so we dismissed the anti-Soviet lies about Stalinist repression.

In the society we hailed as a new human dawn, tens of millions of people were put in slave labor camps, in conditions rivaling Auschwitz and Buchenwald. Between 30 and 40 million people were killed — in peacetime, in the daily routine of socialist rule. While Leftists applauded their progressive policies and guarded their frontiers, Soviet Marxists killed more peasants, more workers and even more Communists, than all the capitalist governments together since the beginning of time.

And for the entire duration of this nightmare, the William Buckleys and Ronald Reagans and the other anti-Communists went on telling the world exactly what was happening. And all that time the pro-Soviet Left and its fellow travelers went on denouncing them as reactionaries and liars, using the same contemptuous terms with which the Left attacks the President today.

In fact, the Left would *still* be denying the Soviet atrocities, if the perpetrators themselves had not finally acknowledged the crimes. In 1956, in a secret speech to the Party elite, Khrushchev made the crimes a Communist fact; but it was only the CIA that actually made the fact public, allowing radicals to come to terms with what they had done. Khrushchev and his cohorts could not have cared less about the misplaced faiths and misspent lives of their naive supporters in the Left. The Soviet rulers were concerned about themselves. Stalin's mania had spread the slaughter into their own ranks. His henchmen wanted to make totalitarianism safe for its rulers. Stalinism without Stalin. In place of a dictator whose paranoia could not be controlled, they instituted a dictatorship by directorate — which (not coincidentally) is the form of rule in Nicaragua today. In the future, Soviet repression would work one way only: from the privileged top of society to the powerless bottom.

The year 1956 — which is also the year Soviet tanks flattened the freedom fighters of Budapest — is the year that tells us who the Sandinistas really are. In this year, because the truth had to be admitted at last, the Left all over the world was forced to redefine itself in relation to the Soviet facts. China's Communist leader, Mao, decided he liked Stalin's way better. For Mao's sinister folly 25 million people died in the "great leaps" and "cultural revolutions" he then launched. But in Europe and America a new anti-Stalinist Left was born. This "New Left," of which I was one of the founders, was repelled by the evils it was now forced to see, and embarrassed by the tarnish the totalitarians had brought to the socialist cause. It turned its back on the Soviet model of Stalin *and* his heirs.

In Nicaragua, the Sandinista vanguard was neither embarrassed nor repelled. The following year, 1957, Carlos Fonseca, the revered founding father of the Sandinista Front, visited Russia and its newly efficient totalitarian state. To Fonseca, as to Borge and his other comrades, the Soviet monstrosity was their revolutionary dream come true. In his pamphlet, *A Nicaraguan in Moscow*, Fonseca proclaimed Soviet Communism his model for Latin America's revolutionary future.

A second step in this vision of a Communist America is now being realized in Nicaragua. The *comandante* directorate, the army and the secret police (socialism's three most important institutions) are already mirrors of the Soviet state — not only structurally but in their personnel, trained and often manned by agents of the Soviet axis.

Yet the most important figure in this transformation is not a Nicaraguan at all, but Cuba's first communist, Fidel Castro. From 1959 when Carlos Fonseca and Tomas Borge first arrived in Havana, and for twenty years after, the Sandinista leaders became disciples of Fidel in Havana, and with his blessings went on to Moscow, where Stalin's henchman completed their revolutionary course. Humberto Ortega, Daniel's less visible but more important brother, is Fidel's personal protege. Ortega is the author of the *tercerista* strategy which allied their minuscule sect to a coalition of democrats contending for power. Fidel is not only the image in which the Sandinista leadership has created itself and the author of its victorious strategy, but the architect of its politburo, the *comandante* directorate. The directorate was personally created by Fidel *in Havana* on the eve of the final struggle, sealed with a pledge of military aid against the Somoza regime. Without Castro's intervention, Arturo Cruz and the other anti-Somoza and pro-democratic Contras would be the government of Nicaragua today.

And it was Fidel who showed the Sandinistas how to steal the revolution after the victory, and how to secure their theft by manipulating their most important allies: the American Left and its liberal sympathizers.

Twenty-five years ago, when the Sandinistas began their apprenticeship, Fidel was our revolutionary hero too. Like today's campus radicals, we became "coffee-pickers" and passengers on the revolutionary tour, wrote glowingly about literacy campaigns, health clinics and other wonders of the new world a-coming. When Fidel spoke, his words were revolutionary music to our ears: "Freedom with bread. Bread without terror." "A revolution neither red nor black, but Cuban olive-green." And so in Managua today: "Not (Soviet) Communism but Nicaraguan *Sandinismo*," is the formula his imitators proclaim.

So persuasive were Fidel's political poems, that radicals all over the world fell under his spell. Jean-Paul Sartre wrote one of the first and most influential books admiring the new leader: "If this man asked me for the moon," the philosopher wrote, "I would give it to him. Because he would have a need for it."

When I listen to today's enthusiasts for the Sandinista redeemers with their scorn for the Contra rebels, the fate of a Fidelista hero comes to my mind, one of the liberators of Cuba, whose role in the revolution was once the equal of Che. For in the year that Jean-Paul Sartre came to Havana and fell in love with the humanitarian Fidel, Huber Matos embarked on a long windowless night of the soul.

Huber Matos' fate began with the second revolution of Fidel. All the fine gestures and words with which Fidel seduced us and won our support — the open Marxism, the socialist humanism, the independent path — were calculated lies. For even as he proclaimed his color to be olive green, he was planning to make his revolution Moscow red. So cynical was Fidel's strategy, that at the time it was difficult for many to comprehend. One by one Fidel removed his own comrades from the revolutionary regime and replaced them with Cuban Communists. At the time, the Communists were a Party in disgrace. They had opposed the revolution; they had even served in the cabinet of the tyrant Batista while the revolution was taking place! But this was all incidental to Fidel.

Fidel knew how to use people. And Fidel was planning a *new* revolution that he could trust the Communists to support. He had decided to turn Cuba into a Soviet state. Moreover, Fidel also knew that he could no longer trust his Fidelista comrades, because they had made a revolution they thought was going to be Cuban olive green.

Although Fidel was a party of one, and the Sandinistas were a party of nine, although he removed socialists and they removed democrats, the pattern of betrayal has been the same in Nicaragua as it was in Cuba: to gain power the Sandinistas concealed their true intention (a Soviet state) behind a revolutionary lie (a pluralist democracy). To consolidate power they fashioned a second lie (democracy, but only within the revolution), and those who believed in the first lie were removed. At the end of the process there will be no democracy in Nicaragua at all, which is exactly what Fonseca and the Sandinistas intended when they began. (When the Sandinistas removed their anti-Somoza allies, of course, they did not need Nicaraguan Communists to replace them. Because they had Fidel behind them, and thousands of agents and technicians from the Communist bloc.)

When Huber Matos saw Fidel's strategy unfolding in Cuba, he got on the telephone with other Fidelistas to discuss what they should do. This was a mistake. In the first year of Cuba's liberation, the phones of revolutionary legends like Huber Matos were already tapped by Fidel's secret police. Huber Matos was arrested.

In the bad old days of Batista oppression, Fidel had been arrested himself. His crime was not words on a telephone, but leading an attack on a military barracks to overthrow the Batista regime. Twelve people were killed. For his offense Fidel spent a total of eighteen months in the tyrant's jail. Huber Matos was not so lucky. Fidel was no Batista, and the revolution was no two-bit dictatorship, like the one it replaced. For his phone call, Huber Matos was tried in such secrecy that not even members of the government were privy to the proceeding. Afterwards, he was consigned to solitary confinement in a windowless cell for the next twenty-two years. And even as Fidel buried his former friend and comrade alive, he went on singing his songs of revolutionary humanism and social justice.

In another context, Milan Kundera explains the meaning of this revolutionary parable of Huber Matos and Fidel. Recalling the French Communist, Paul Eluard, who wrote poems praising brotherhood while his friend was murdered by Eluard's comrades in Communist Prague, Kundera remarked: "The hangman killed while the poet sang." He explained these words thus: "People like to say: Revolution is beautiful, it is only the terror arising from it which is evil. But this is not true. The evil is already present in the beautiful, hell is already contained in the dream of paradise....To condemn gulags is easy, but to reject the totalitarian poetry which leads to the gulag by way of paradise is as difficult as ever." Words to bear in mind today as we consider Nicaragua and its revolution of poets.

To believe in the revolutionary dream is the tragedy of its supporters; to exploit the dream is the talent of its dictators. Revolutionary cynicism, the source of this talent, is Fidel's most important teaching to his Sandinista disciples. This is the faculty that allows the *comandantes* to emulate Fidel himself: to be poets and hangmen at the same time. To promise democracy and organize repression, to attack imperialism and join an empire, to talk peace and plan war, to champion justice and to deliver Nicaragua to a fraternity of inhumane, repressive, militarized and economically crippled states.

"We used to have one main prison, now we have many," — thus begins the lament of a former Fidelista for the paradise that Nicaragua has now gained. "We used to have a few barracks; now we have many. We used to have many plantations; now we have only one, and it belongs to Fidel. Who enjoys the fruits of the revolution? The houses of the rich, the luxuries of the rich? The *Comandante* and his court."

Nicaragua is now in the grip of utterly cynical and utterly ruthless men whose purpose is to crush its society from top to bottom, to institute totalitarian rule, and to use Nicaragua as a base to spread Communist terror and regimes throughout the hemisphere. The Sandinista anthem which proclaims the Yankee to be the "enemy of mankind" expresses precisely the revolutionaries' sentiment and goal. That goal is hardly to create new societies — the sordid record of Communist states would dissuade any reformer from choosing the Communist path — but to destroy the societies that already exist.

For Nicaragua, a Contra victory would mean the restoration of the democratic leadership from whom the Sandinistas stole the revolution, the government that Nicaragua would have had if Cuba had not intervened in the first place. For the Americas, it would mean a halt in the Communist march that threatens its freedoms and its peace. Support for the Contras is a first line of defense. If they fail, it will hasten the time when Americans will have to defend themselves.

*   *   *

A final word to my former comrades and successors in the Left: it is no accident that the greatest atrocities in the 20th Century have been committed by Marxist radicals; and it is no accident that they have been committed by radicals in power against their own peoples. Hatred of self, and by extension one's country, is the root of the radical cause. As American radicals, the most egregious sin you commit is to betray the privileges and freedoms ordinary people from all over the world have come to this country to create — privileges and freedoms that ordinary people all over the world would feel blessed to have themselves. But the worst of it is this: that you betray all of this tangible good that you can see around you, for a socialist-pie-in-the-sky that has meant horrible deaths and miserable lives for the hundreds of millions who have already fallen under its sway. ☐

Chapter Three

Cuba Then, Nicaragua Now

(Peter Collier & David Horowitz)

A specter is haunting Congress — the specter of revolutions past and their graveyards of good intentions. Ever since the Bolsheviks seized power in 1917, starry-eyed Leftists and well-meaning liberals in the West joined forces to provide new Marxist regimes with vitally needed breathing space and support. Recognizing the importance of their efforts, Trotsky called them the "frontier guards" of the revolution. As Congress debates the President's request for aid to the Nicaraguan Contras, and today's frontier guards lobby for "fair play" for yet another experiment in Marxist social planning, it is important to remember how people with seemingly good intentions have continuously supported these revolutions whose record of success is so consistently appalling.

For three generations the "progressive Left" has endorsed and abetted the most murderous, repressive and economically disastrous social experiments of the 20th Century. In the name of "social justice" successive "popular fronts" of radicals and liberals have lent support to regimes featuring slave labor, politically induced famines, mass executions, and ethnic genocide on a scale unmatched in human history. At intermittent points the bankruptcy of Marxism and the catastrophes of Communist practice have stripped the scales from believers' eyes causing momentary liberal retreats and defections by a chastened few; but the diehards remain, eternally innocent and willfully ignorant. They learn nothing and forget everything as they move on to the newest revolution and the next popular front, while their ranks are continually swelled by the born yesterday and the born again.

Since Marxism's first triumph, the campaigns of the frontier guards in the West have never varied. The objective is always the same: to buy

A Policy Forum Paper of the National Forum Foundation, 1986.

time for the new rulers until they consolidate their power (and after which it no longer matters how brazenly their ruthlessness is displayed). Since only the votes of democratic parliaments can realize this objective, the campaign strategy is also always the same: to prick the guilty conscience of the West and to paralyze the democratic will to resist. Thus when the Bolsheviks' early despotism betrayed their lethal intent and the West responded, the frontier guards sprang to the revolutions' defense by shifting the onus of blame: Bolshevik oppression was *caused* by its opponents and the West's intervention was but a new imperialist ploy. The remedy they proposed: the democracies must cut off their aid to the counter-revolutionary forces and give the revolution a chance.

"Counter-revolutionaries" then, Contras now: what the frontier guards want is the same — a peace that will consolidate Marxist rule. They are powerfully abetted in the present instance by the lingering crisis of identity and will that followed America's defeat in Vietnam. For this defeat has left a canker of paralyzing doubt in the minds of many committed democrats who now question the efficacy and morality of using American power to defend democracy abroad. The frontier guards have no such commitment to democratic principle, but a cynical appreciation of their opportunity in America's guilt which is unfailing and acute. Their plea in behalf of the latest band of totalitarians to seize control of a hapless country reverberates in the current congressional debates. Their argument against aid to the Contras appeals to two propositions which shrewdly recall a "mini-Vietnam" in the hemisphere itself:

(1) The United States must avoid in Nicaragua the mistake made in Cuba where U.S. intervention and opposition to Castro forced him into the arms of the Soviet Union. (2) By supporting the Contra's fight against so-called "early signs of totalitarianism" in the Sandinista regime, we will surely drive them towards it. (And, by the same logic, encourage them to export revolution as a means of "defending" their own.)

This argument recognizes the genetic connection between the first Marxist base in the hemisphere and the second, but fails to understand its significance. For once this connection is understood the argument becomes absurd.

Long ago Castro constructed a Soviet mini-state in Cuba, purging the last vestiges of its freedom, and submerging Cuban society in a long totalitarian night. At the same time he made himself a global agent of Soviet imperialism and Cuba a Soviet base. Far from hiding his imperialist zeal, Castro expressed it as publicly and enthusiastically in supporting the Red Army's re-conquest of Czechoslovakia in 1968, as he does now in applauding its genocidal aggression in Afghanistan. But his greatest service to Soviet power has been in providing a mercenary force for its expansion in far-flung places like Angola and Ethiopia, where his troops make possible a sadistic Marxist rule that has caused famine and suffering on a vast human scale.

Now put this together with the fact that in programmatic statements both public and private and in declarations both informal and official, the Sandinista rulers of Nicaragua have proclaimed Castro and his Cuba to be their revolutionary model. Totalitarianism is the *aim* of the current Nicaraguan regime, not its last resort. Which is why men like Eden Pastora, the guerrilla hero of the anti-Somoza rebellion and anti-Somoza political leaders like Alfonso Robelo and Arturo Cruz are now exiled leaders of the Contras. Since Cuba is the model for the Sandinistas and their aim is a Communist state (and — make no mistake — their wish is for a Communist juggernaut throughout the hemisphere), it is ludicrous to contend that U.S. support for anti-Communist forces is driving them in a totalitarian direction.

A similar contention provides the second pillar of the argument against taking strong action against the Sandinista threat. What about this premise that the United States was historically responsible for Cuba's embrace of Soviet totalitarianism in the first place?

As a formula it provides a staple position for those on the Left for whom the United States can do no right. America is blamed first for the oppressive situations that produce revolutionaries like Castro, and then for the brutal "solutions" the Castros produce. Yet the argument also seems to have wide currency among others whose criticism has more honorable intent.

To sustain it, however, requires standing historical reality on its head. For the testimony of Fidelistas disillusioned by Castro's perversion and betrayal of their revolution has by now made the thesis untenable. Most prominent among the testimonies is the remarkable memoir of Carlos Franqui who was at Castro's side in the Sierra Maestra and whom he personally designated to write the revolution's history. Franqui's recollections irrevocably lift the veil of deception with which Fidel masked his early intentions.

A far more subtle and accomplished political manipulator than his Sandinista disciples, Castro had initially criticized both socialism and capitalism and proclaimed his revolution to be independent of the Cold War blocs. This later lent substance to the illusion that he turned to the Soviets reluctantly and only under U.S. pressure. Yet Franqui's account of Castro's role in the internal struggles of the revolution leave no doubt that his famous proclamations were so much dust thrown into everyone's eyes. Far from being driven reluctantly into waiting Soviet arms, Fidel actively *provoked* and escalated the confrontation with Washington *in order* to force a cautious, apprehensive and recalcitrant Kremlin to grant that embrace. The reason for his eagerness in seeking Soviet protection was not to defend Cuba and its "olive green" revolution against U.S. assault, but because his *intention* from pre-revolutionary days (evidenced even in his conduct of the guerrilla campaigns) was to turn Cuba into a Soviet-style Communist state.

Like most of its supporters, Franqui had joined Fidel's 26th of July Movement believing that Fidel meant what he said and that under his leadership Cuba was going to pursue a socialist path different from the oppressive collectivisms of the Soviet bloc. Yet as soon as Fidel was in power, other intentions became evident. The Cuban Communist Party had opposed the revolution to the very last minute, even participating in the cabinet of the Batista dictatorship. But the moment victory was won Castro systematically began to place Cuban Communists in control of the strategic offices of the revolution, and just as systematically to dismantle and destroy all the indigenous Left organizations — his own 26th of July Movement, the free and socialist trade union movement, and the non-Communist socialist press.

Even as he was changing the personnel of the revolution he was altering its institutional direction: "Some of Fidel's decisions bothered us: state-owned farms [very much like those sending up malign blooms in Nicaragua today] instead of self-regulating cooperative farms. We wanted small-scale agriculture so that we would not be substituting for the old boss a new administrator, for the old owner a new, state owner. But Fidel had an innate distrust of the people; he preferred militarization to organization...." Since he had little indigenous support for this program, aside from the discredited Communists, he was forced to improvise. The year in Cuba is 1960, *prior* to the Bay of Pigs: "Fidel's strategy was to compromise the Soviet Union by rapidly deploying the structures of the Soviet state — the Communist Party and a State Security agency. But even the Soviet government was unwilling to comply... All Soviet emissaries, ambassadors — even Khrushchev and Mikoyan — recommended calm and patience. They were all shocked at the accelerated and artificial process of nationalization they saw us engaged in. The more they worried, the faster Fidel went. He envisioned a new kind of government — a Russian structure, but with himself at the top..." (Carlos Franqui, *Family Portrait With Fidel*, p.78)

With these realities of Cuba's past firmly in focus, the Nicaraguan picture becomes sharp and clear as well. In 1961, as Fidel accelerated his program of Sovietization in Cuba, three Nicaraguan Marxists made a political pilgrimage to Havana, and founded the FSLN — the Sandinista vanguard that controls Nicaragua today. The first among these three, the recognized father of *Sandinismo*, Carlos Fonseca, had written a book four years earlier called *A Nicaraguan in Moscow*, which portrayed the Soviet Union as the model of the revolutionary future for all Latin America. It was only natural therefore that he and his comrades — Silvio Mayorga and Tomas Borge (Nicaragua's current Minister of the Interior) — should return to Cuba again and again over the years as eager proteges of its Communist *caudillo* and as worshipers at the altars of his emerging Soviet state. These were the original "Sandinista" leaders, the forerunners; but they were followed by the Ortega brothers and all the other *comandantes* of the present Sandinista directorate, not only to Castro's school in Havana, but on to Moscow — the avowed mecca of their revolutionary ideals. Over the course of a decade, Moscow and Havana were literally their political schools. At the feet of Castro and of the Brezhnevs and Andropovs, they acquired skills in weaponry and Stalinist theory, and accumulated the tools for building a totalitarian state.

But while accumulating accolades in the Communist capitals they failed to make much headway in Nicaragua itself. Their guerrilla forces languished in the hinterlands with little popular support, a situation that continued up to a year before their triumph. And like all Marxist mini-sects they split into factions (three to be exact), making their guerrilla forces weaker still. This was the state of affairs in March 1979 when the Somoza regime began to visibly weaken. Seeing that his disciples' fractiousness was jeopardizing their opportunity, Castro stepped directly into the picture, intervening in the internal events of Nicaragua in a way that Jimmy Carter, paralyzed by misconstrued lessons of Vietnam, dared not.

Perceiving that the combined pressures of Carter's human rights policy and Nicaraguan democrats had pushed Somoza's deteriorating position to a critical stage, and realizing that, few as they were, his disciples united would make the strongest armed anti-Somoza force, Castro summoned them to Havana for an offer they couldn't refuse: Cuba's military support for unification. Under Castro's guiding hand, the three factions became one. And on March 7, 1979 the present ruling "Sandinista Directorate" was born in Havana with Castro's favorite, most Stalinist and most ruthless disciples — Defense Minister Humberto Ortega and Interior Minister Tomas Borge its dominant *comandantes*.

Castro's success in Nicaragua is more than an incidental ambition, since — like every other Marxist ruler — he has failed so miserably and completely in his own country to realize his revolutionary goals. Cuba is more abjectly dependent on a foreign power and its population more materially deprived than it was when he first took power. Like every Marxist revolutionary before him, he has dealt with this failure by instituting a police state so ruthless and pervasive that the cries of suffering at all levels of Cuban society will be stifled before they can erupt in political protest. To pay for the vast Soviet subsidy to his bankrupt economy, and to rekindle his fading revolutionary star, Castro has turned Cuba into a base for the KGB and the Soviet military. Cuba's 225,000 man army and advanced Soviet weaponry make it the second most powerful military force in the Western Hemisphere. With nearly 50,000 combatant troops in Africa, and with deep political and logistical involvements in terrorist movements in Central America and the

Caribbean, Cuba is a spawning ground of totalitarian influences and a source of constant instability across the globe.

* * *

Whatever the pious promises of the Sandinista regime, with Castro as its father and Cuba its model, the reasonable and prudent assumption is of a similar development in Nicaragua if the Sandinista's present stranglehold on the population should be consolidated. If this blow to democracy and freedom were to occur, Nicaragua will take its place alongside Cuba as a base of Soviet power and a staging ground of Communist expansion. One can imagine those who oppose aid to the anti-Communist forces now saying twenty years hence, when it has become impossible even for them to deny the despotism and menace of the Sandinista state, that it was all the fault of the United States, which drove them to evil back in the time when in fact the Contras offered the only alternative to Nicaragua's totalitarian fate. □

Chapter Four

Boiling the Sea in Afghanistan

(Peter Collier)

Others may worry about U.S. involvement in Central America, but Dr. Robert Simon is one of those who wonders why we are not in Afghanistan. One of sixteen children of an immigrant Lebanese laborer whose name, Hussein Abdul Jalil, was changed to Hassan Simon by officials at Ellis Island, the 34 year old Simon never had much time for causes while he was getting through medical school and working in his specialty — emergency medicine — in upstate Michigan. Early last winter, however, after four years as a professor at the UCLA Medical School, Simon began reading about the growing medical crisis in Afghanistan. He found that tuberculosis, which had been so well controlled before the 1979 Russian invasion that there were only 20 beds devoted to it at Kabul University Medical School, now afflicts 135 people per 1000; that malaria, which the World Health Organization had termed a negligible problem in Afghanistan before the Russians' arrival, now affects 50 per 1000; that whooping cough, measles, dysentery and other diseases have reached epidemic proportions.

Probing the situation more deeply, Simon read Dutch journalists' accounts of the Soviets' chemical warfare against the rural population in Afghanistan, and Amnesty International reports on the effects of torture by the Kabul government's KGB-trained secret police. But what finally caused him to decide to go to Afghanistan was the discovery that Western-trained physicians there had been virtually eliminated and that the Russians had systematically destroyed the medical facilities established in the 85% of the countryside which is controlled by the *mujaheddin* freedom fighters.

A Policy Forum *paper of the National Forum Foundation, June 1985.*

Simon thought it would be easy for a physician to volunteer his services through established international health organizations. But when he contacted the World Health Organization and the International Red Cross, these organizations, which had been able to maintain presences in Vietnam, Lebanon and other politically sensitive war zones, told him that the Russian puppet government in Kabul had forbidden them from operating in the country. Planning a leave of absence from UCLA, Simon searched for other ways to penetrate the medical iron curtain. Finally, he contacted a group called the Union of Mujaheddin Doctors which helped him make arrangements, and, after several months of preparation, he took a leave of absence and went to Afghanistan early last summer.

After a week in Pakistan gathering supplies and meeting with *mujaheddin* commanders who came over the border to see him, Simon, in a turban and robe like his bodyguards and the bearers carrying medical supplies donated by a Swedish relief agency, entered Afghanistan through a remote mountain pass north of Peshawar, the first American physician to travel there since the Russian takeover.

Stopping only to hide from Soviet planes, the party walked 15 miles a day in 110 degree temperatures until they reached Konar Province. There Simon set up a clinic in a camouflaged tent, and protected by a captured Russian anti-aircraft gun and a *mujaheddin* serving as a "triage officer," began work on the sick and wounded who had travelled up to 50 miles — always at night to avoid being spotted by helicopter gunships — to see him. A donkey was the ambulance. Folding cots served as operating tables. Twelve sleeping bags were the hospital beds. When he ran out of gesso for plaster casts, Simon used the mud and straw mix the people used to build houses. When he ran out of sutures, he sterilized hair from the tail of a mule and used that. When he ran out of that he told them to grit their teeth. After he had pulled shrapnel out of gangrenous wounds and treated villagers for such diseases as malaria and meningitis, they often gave him an egg or a cup of goat's milk in payment.

As he worked, Simon was told of whole villages whose population had been herded into irrigation tunnels and incinerated by gasoline fires as Soviet troops applauded from above; of uncooperative village elders being forced to stay outside during the freezing nights and losing fingers and toes to frostbite as a result; of children having their throats slit in front of their parents.

What he saw in his own patients convinced him that there was little exaggeration in these stories. One of his cases was a boy who had been doused with kerosene and then set afire by Soviet troops when he refused to tell where *mujaheddin* were hiding. Simon also treated villagers who had lost legs to the anti-personnel devices strewn by airdrop across the countryside; children who had lost a hand or part of their face to the booby-trapped devices in the shape of toy trucks and butterflies, which the Soviet troops had strategically placed to capture their attention; people suffering from the aftermath of chemical attacks which had destroyed lungs, caused bleeding from all orifices, and softened the flesh so that it pulled away from the bone like overdone meat.

By the end of his several weeks in Afghanistan, Simon had begun asking himself a question that his next several months working for the cause of Afghanistan at home would leave unanswered: "The Russians are committing atrocities that rank with those of Nazi Germany. Why is it that we and the rest of the world are once again standing by and watching it happen?"

Perhaps part of the problem is that Afghanistan seems so far away, not only spatially but conceptually as well — a 19th century Kiplingesque world of empire and romance, of ambushes and alarms in austere mountain passes. The *mujaheddin* freedom fighters are backward in the ways of Western media, and have never mastered the capacity for projecting stirring images of themselves and their struggle as the Indochinese once did and some Central Americans now do.

The notion of guerrillas in turbans and sandals who follow the injunction of the Koran rather than those of a home-brewed Marxism ("Do not accept the orders of the infidels; wage *jihad* against them.") and who go off to fight against tanks and planes armed in some cases with nothing more than World War I bolt action rifles suggests an inscrutable, almost foolhardy, bravery. Indeed, some stories of their courage which have escaped the news blackout the Russians have drawn like a noose around the country (Dr. Simon, for instance, tells of meeting the freedom fighter who lost a leg to a mine and, after being fitted with an artificial one, asked his commander if he could function as a human mine detector because he had only half as much to lose as one of his comrades) seem so extreme as to be on the edge of the grotesque.

Yet the fact is that however distant it may seem, however antique and eccentric, Afghanistan is a place to which the word *genocide* can be applied without diluting its special historical significance. A nation that was a net exporter of wheat and dried fruit before the 1979 invasion, it is now so impoverished that a British medical team recently smuggled into the countryside estimates that up to one half million people now suffer from malnutrition and could die of starvation.

Of the approximately 16 million people in the country in 1980, an estimated one million have been killed and wounded since the coming of the Red Army. Soviet terror has created some four million refugees, better than one-quarter of the nation - two and a half million in Pakistan and one and a half in Iran. These figures do not even count the "internal" refugees — the hundreds of thousands of villagers forced to leave their scorched earth for the Russian-controlled big cities which are the only places where food is available, or the tens of thousands of school children sent off to the Soviet Union to be educated as cadre and reinfiltrated into Afghanistan later on as spies and assassins.

Soviet strategy in Afghanistan is based on a brutal rejoinder to Mao's poetic notion of guerrillas as fish swimming in the sea of popular support. If that is so, Russian generals answer, then we shall boil that sea and ultimately drain it, leaving the fish exposed and gasping on barren land. In 1980, during the initial arrogance of an invasion which presumed little resistance, Soviet ground forces assaulted villages in search and destroy actions. But after these troops began taking heavy causalities, the Russians made the transition to an air war of attrition featuring MIGs and helicopter gunships, carpet bombings and the deadly "yellow rain" which even the Left-leaning People's Tribunal in Paris (successor to the Bertrand Russell War Crimes Tribunal) has affirmed is being used in Afghanistan.

The military objective is terror rather than victory per se. This campaign of bombed-out villages and anti-personnel devices is based on the cold insight that an injured person is more trouble than a dead one to a guerrilla organization, not only trouble to transport and care for, but trouble too when comrades must watch him suffer and die horribly from gangrene or the violent staph infections which ultimately kill most of the seriously wounded.

It is this emphasis on terror and attrition that has made the destruction of medical facilities in the countryside a key element of Soviet strategy. Before 1978, according to Dr. Jameel Zicria, a professor of Surgery at Columbia University Hospital and the contact with the Union of Mujaheddin Doctors who helped arrange Simon's trip, there were some 1,400 physicians in Afghanistan, two-thirds of them Western-trained. Now, after purges, murders and flight, he estimates that there are perhaps 200 left, almost all of them centered in the large cities which constitute the 15% of the country under Russian control.

The network of clinics by which the old medical infrastructure extended medical care into the countryside have long since been destroyed by Russian bombing. When the courageous French organization *Medecins Sans Frontieres* made its way into Afghanistan to remedy this lack by equipping several field hospitals, four of them (according to MSF Executive Director Dr. Claude Malhuret) were bombed by Soviet planes despite red crosses painted on their roofs, and two others had to be evacuated.

The net result is that not only the freedom fighters themselves but the hundreds of thousands of peasants caught in the Soviets' gunsights must travel to the Pakistan border for medical attention, hoping they make it to one of the International Red Cross ambulances waiting impotently there for the wounded to leave the country. It is not only because of their ability to heal that doctors are excluded from Afghanistan but also because they are potential witnesses to the barbarity taking place there. "The Soviets are trying to terrorize the population into submission," says Dr. Robert Simon, "and they don't want medical people around because they know that doctors will be the first to see the evidence of the atrocities they're committing."

Why is it then that the extermination and dispersal of a people has not gained more attention and sympathy? Part of the reason may be the coercive power of an analogy. Afghanistan is, we are constantly told, Russia's Vietnam. Those who say this seem to think that by simply making the association they have doomed the Soviet war effort. Actually, the analogy is based on a misunderstanding of what Vietnam was and what Afghanistan is. Most obviously, Vietnam was a high-tech television war; Afghanistan is one of those old fashioned encounters that takes place in the dark. There is no such thing as independent media in the Soviet Union able to question whether or not there is light at the end of the tunnel; no cameras bringing back nightly footage that shows the brutality visited on an innocent people or the body bags offloading from Soviet transport; no reports of growing revulsion on the homefront, no protests in the street or clamor to bring the boys home.

Afghanistan is not Vietnam because the people committing atrocities never *see* them. Nor do people in the rest of the world, for it is not only their own news organizations that the Russians have been able to censor. Without access to the imagery of the war, much of the international press has assumed that the *mujaheddin* have not mounted a compelling resistance, although on the rare occasions when they manage to get into the country they find quite the contrary. For instance, a Sunday London *Times* writer who took advantage of a bureaucratic lapse to lay over in Kabul on a flight to Moscow found that the capital was a "city besieged" with Soviet troops under assault day and night, with children openly selling Russians drugs, with a 100-vehicle Russian convoy attacked by *mujaheddin* a half mile from the Intercontinental Hotel where he was staying. By the laws of political entropy, however, the relative lack of such reports seems to mitigate against there being such news in the future.

Another reason why the Vietnam analogy doesn't work is that the Soviets don't care whether or not they win the hearts and minds of the people, as long as they win. The analogy breaks down even more fundamentally on the fact that the Afghanistan resistance has no super-power ally willing to support and underwrite their war effort, as the Vietnamese did. And so the truth of the Vietnam analogy is not that guerrillas will ultimately defeat a superpower, but that a war against an indigenous population not waged under the high intensity microscope of a free press and a sensitivity to world opinion is eminently winnable. Indeed, there is evidence that Red Army generals are actually enjoying the opportunity to allow certain of their units to be "blooded" in this conflict, which has already lasted longer than Russian involvement in World War II.

It is also clear that the Soviets count on the double standard which seems to exist in the rest of the free world when it comes time to measure their actions against those of the United States. Grenada brings demonstrations in all the major capitals of Europe; the anniversaries of Afghanistan are marked by a handful of emigres holding vigils in front of the Russian embassies. In a recent speech on world affairs, Sweden's Olaf Palme mentioned U.S. involvement in Central America 53 times and Soviet involvement in Afghanistan once.

Even more incomprehensibly, this double standard seems to exist also in the U.S. media and intellectual community. The Sandinistas' anti-American propaganda is given credibility by all the major news gathering organizations; the war in Afghanistan is virtually ignored. Particularly after Dan Rather was ridiculed by his colleagues as "Gunga Dan" for having gone into Afghanistan in native robes and headdress, few television correspondents have bothered to go into that country for first-hand reports; the networks back home don't even bother to carry footage smuggled out by European camera crews.

The same groups who warn that 60 U.S. advisers in El Salvador or Administration concerns over Soviet weapons flows into Nicaragua presages invasions there, "explain" the accomplished invasion and occupation of Afghanistan by 120,000 troops as a matter of legitimate Soviet strategic concerns. The same groups who support self-determination for the Sandinistas deny that support to the *mujaheddin* because they don't possess radical chic. Because anti-Soviet attitudes are involved, Afghanistan is dismissed as a dowdy conservative issue; Central America is appealing because it embodies the anti-American attitudes which continue to exist in this culture at a level untouched by the "renewal of patriotism."

The U.S. continues to pick the scab of Vietnam and bleed a politics of guilty impotence while Afghanistan dies. Afghanistan should matter not just because of narrow strategic issues, although denying the Soviets access to their long-range imperial goals involving the Indian Subcontinent and the Persian Gulf, goals which are predicated on the conquest of Afghanistan, seem laudable enough. Afghanistan should matter to us for reasons which shouldn't even have to be mentioned — because the *mujaheddin* are a brave people fighting against a tyrannical invader; because their cause is an opportunity to place this country on the right side in a war of national liberation.

We are occasionally given to understand that we are covertly aiding the *mujaheddin* through the CIA. The aid ought to be overt, a matter of national pride as well as national policy. In the same spirit that we try to alleviate Ethiopian famine, we ought to be sending hand-held missile launchers and other weapons to end the Soviet reign of terror from the air and to be collecting blood and other supplies to forestall the medical catastrophe which is one aspect of Soviet strategy for the country. That we are *not* only not doing these things but not even talking about Afghanistan is a mystery to someone like Dr. Robert Simon.

In the months since returning from Afghanistan he has founded the International Medical Corps, an organization meant to remedy the fact that world medical aid groups have been excluded from that country by the Soviets. His aim is to raise nearly $2 million which would not only help train a corps of native paramedics based on the "barefoot doctors" of China, but also staff eight medical-surgical clinics to be placed in caves safe from Soviet rockets and bombs, each with an American and native doctor, a nurse and two orderlies. But it is hard going. Right now Simon goes around with his slide show comprised of images of his visit, performing before politicians and public service groups.

So far the support is lukewarm. The Sandinistas are a far trendier cause on the lucrative Hollywood cocktail circuit. The State Department professes approval for the goals of the International Medical Corps but warns that "incidents" involving American doctors as potential hostages could create embarrassing situations. All this puzzles Simon, as well it might. "It isn't like supporting the Vietnamese was," he says. "The *mujaheddin* just want the supplies. They'll do the rest by themselves. Right now they're holding out against a superpower using Nazi tactics.

But if we continue to ignore them they're going to be exterminated."
☐

Chapter Five

Reality And Dream

(David Horowitz)

I was born fifty years ago in 1939, just before the Germans invaded Poland. This is my first trip to your country and it has been inspiring to me to see that although you have been occupied for half a century you have not been defeated.

The members of my family were socialists for more than 100 years; first in Moravia and the Ukraine, then in New York and Berkeley. First as socialists; then as Communists; and then as New Left Marxists. My grandparents came to New York to escape persecution as Jews in the pale of settlement. My grandfather was a tailor. He lived with other Jews in poverty on the Lower East Side and earned three dollars a week. He was so poor that sometimes he had to sleep under his sewing machine in the factory where he worked. Compared to czarist Russia from which he had fled, America was a new world: he was still poor, but he had arrived in a land of opportunities provided by its free market economy and political democracy, a land where people could grow rich beyond their wildest dreams.

* * *

That was my grandfather's reality. Like many others who arrived in America, my grandfather also had a dream. His dream, however, was not a dream of riches. It was a dream he shared with other members of the International Left: the dream of a socialist future — a world of planned economy and economic equality, of material abundance and social justice. In 1917, my grandfather thought he saw his dream become reality in Bolshevik Russia.

Text of a talk delivered at the Second Thoughts Conference *in Cracow, Poland, May 4-7, 1989, just before Poland became free.*

By this time, my grandfather had had a son. Like the children of other immigrant families, his son studied and worked hard to take advantage of the opportunities provided by America's freedom. He became a high school teacher and married a colleague, and also had a son. By this time, my father was no longer poor like his father, but middle-class. He and my mother could afford culture, travel, an automobile and a grand piano. In 1949, with their school teachers' salaries they bought a six-room house on credit for $18,000. In 1986, when my father died, the house belonged to him, as his property. It was worth $200,000. That was my father's reality: riches and freedom beyond *his* father's wildest dreams.

But like his father, mine also had his heart set on a different dream than the freedom and wealth that America had made possible for him. Just as his father had been a Socialist, my father was a Communist. He supported the "experiment" that Lenin and Stalin had begun in Soviet Russia. All his life he dreamed the Communist future, and he transmitted that dream to his son.

In 1956, events occurred in Moscow and in Eastern Europe that almost made me give up the dream I had inherited as my family birthright. In 1956, the head of the Soviet Communist Party, Nikita Khrushchev, gave his secret speech on the "crimes of Stalin" and thus drew aside a piece of the veil that had concealed from the faithful the grim reality of the socialist future. Soviet tanks thundered across the border to crush the brave forces of the Hungarian Revolution and to discourage the hopeful beginnings of the Polish October.

Instead of being awakened by these events, I joined a new generation who hoped to revive the humanist spirit of the dream itself. I was inspired to join the New Left by a Polish Marxist named Isaac Deutscher, who was my teacher. It was Deutscher who devised the theory out of which we hoped to revive the socialist dream.

According to Deutscher, the Stalinist state that had murdered millions and erected an edifice of totalitarian lies was a deformation of the socialist ideal that socialists themselves would overcome. The socialist revolution had taken place in the "backward environment" of czarist Russia. Stalinism was a form of "primitive socialist accumulation" produced by the cultural backwardness of that environment and the political necessities of building an industrial economic base.

In 1956, when Khrushchev launched the process of de-Stalinization, Deutscher saw it as the prelude to the humanist future of which we all had dreamed. The socialist economic base — infinitely superior in rationality and productive potential to its capitalist competitor — had already been created. Socialist accumulation had been completed; the socialist superstructure would follow in due course. Socialist abundance would produce socialist democracy.

When we heard words like these, New Leftists all over the world became new believers in the socialist cause. Stalinism had been terrible, but the terror was over. The socialist economic base had been built in Russia. To complete the dream, all that was required was political democracy. In the New Left in the Sixties, we had a saying: *The first socialist revolution will take place in the Soviet Union.* Some Leftists are still saying it today.

For seventeen years, I waited in vain for the democratic revolution to come to Soviet Russia, to complete the socialist dream. But it did not come. Oh, there was a spring in Prague. But Soviet tanks again rolled across the border to crush it. Five years later, another Polish Marxist — now ex-Marxist— stepped forward to explain why socialism would never be realized except in a totalitarian state. In 1956, Leszek Kolakowski had been a leader of the Polish October. In 1968, Kolakowski had been a defender of the Prague spring. Now, in 1973, at a conference in England, Kolakowski summed up 100 years of critiques of socialism that history had repeatedly confirmed: the effort to transform natural inequalities into social equality could only lead to greater, more brutal inequality; the socialist effort to transform individual diversity into social unity could only lead to the totalitarian state.

Deutscher was wrong. There would never be a socialist political democracy erected on a socialist economic base. Socialism was an impossible — and therefore destructive — dream.

But if Kolakowski was right, the future of peoples who lived under socialism was dark indeed. The totalitarian empire could not reform, but it could expand. Aided by dreamers all over the world, the expansion of that empire seemed likely, even inevitable.

* * *

Until now, the era of *glasnost*. Now, instead of a continuing expansion, we see Communism everywhere in retreat. Now, its believers are fewer and fewer, and the terrain itself is beginning to shrink. Yet, who among us expected this? A year and a half ago, I participated in an international panel in Paris which discussed the question: Is Communism reversible? No member of the panel thought it was. This year, if a similar panel were held, the question would be: Can Communism save itself? Who would be so bold to say that it can?

Why were we so wrong? Because all of us, Kolakowski included, had our roots in the intellectual traditions of the socialist Left. Experience had taught us all to be anti-Communist, but our critique of socialism was based on *political* theory and *political* considerations. We knew that totalitarianism was evil, but we thought that socialism worked. We were wrong. It does not work. Economically, it cannot succeed.

While we were wrong, others all along had been right. All those years, outside the socialist tradition, there had been voices crying in the wilderness saying that not only would socialism bring tyranny and suffering, it would not work. Seventy-seven years ago, five years after the Bolshevik triumph, Ludwig von Mises wrote a book on socialism which predicted the catastrophe we see before us. Socialist economy, he argued, was economic irrationality, and socialist planning a prescription for chaos. Only a capitalist market could provide a system of rational allocations and rational accounts. Only private property and the profit motive could unleash the forces of individual initiative and human creativity to produce real and expanding wealth — not only for the rich, but for society as a whole.

Ludwig von Mises, Friedrich von Hayek, and the other liberal theorists of a free market economy who warned of this outcome, are the true prophets of the reality we see before us — of socialist bankruptcy and Communist retreat. *Glastnost*ian democracy has not (and cannot) complete the socialist dream; it can only expose this dream as a nightmare from which Communism cannot wake up. The only way to wake up is to give up the dream. In 1989, according to Soviet economists, the average Soviet citizen had a daily ration of meat that was smaller than the daily intake of the average Russian *in 1913* under the czar. Socialism makes men poor beyond their wildest dreams. The average Polish citizen is poorer today, in 1989, than my poor grandfather was in America, fifty years ago, when I was born.

The law of socialist economy is this: from each according to his exploitability to the *nomenklatura* according to its greed. Not only does the socialist economy not produce wealth at the rate a free economy does, the socialist economy consumes wealth. It consumes both the natural wealth of the nation and the wealth it has accumulated in the past. Every Communist revolution begins as a rape of the present and continues as a cannibalization of the past. Every Communist Party is the colonizer of its own country and the Soviet empire is the colonizer of them all. That is the law of socialist distribution: from each nation according to its exploitability, to the empire according to its greed.

But a system that lives by cannibalism, that consumes more wealth than it produces, is sooner or later destined to die. And that is what is happening before our eyes.

For myself, my family tradition of socialist dreams is over. Socialism is no longer a dream of the revolutionary future. It is only a nightmare of the past. But for you, the nightmare is not a dream. It is a reality that is still happening. My dream for the people of socialist Poland is that someday soon you will wake up from your nightmare, and be free. □

Chapter Six

May Day Reflections, 1990

(Peter Collier)

Those of you who have done some writing may recognize a writer's trick in the title I have chosen for this speech. Call something a "reflection" and you escape responsibility for constructing a rigorous narrative strategy. Anything is a reflection. But have patience. These reflections do have a coherence. Some of you might not like it, but it is there.

Twenty years ago, when I was still a radical, I would have been aware of May Day primarily as a day when Red Square was filled with the ponderous military might of the Soviet war machine. At that time, this phenomenon did not bother me. In fact, it was vaguely reassuring. One of the great innovations of the New Left in the Sixties was the idea that Leftism should not be pro-Soviet, but rather anti-American. I did not really support the U.S.S.R. *per se.* The Soviet Union was not a very appealing country, and even the revisionism of the Sixties could not change that. Rather, my comrades and I regarded the U.S.S.R. in the same way one might regard the brainless bully who happens to be in your corner during the street fight. The Soviet Union was, we thought, the ultimate guarantor of world revolution. However unpalatable the Soviet experience of Communism might be, the U.S.S.R. nonetheless stood behind places like Havana and Hanoi where we believed Utopia was being born. We radicals did not really like those missiles being paraded in Red Square, but the fact that they were aimed against the U.S. made them okay.

That was then and this is now. For me that dream of socialist Utopia has long since faded, faded to the extent that I have come to see those who continue to dream it as being — in one of the obscene catch phrases

Speech given at Macalester College, St. Paul, May 1, 1990.

that has been around since 1917 — enemies of the people. And May Day 1990 itself is a different observance. Soviet tanks no longer have the capacity to support revolution, but only to intimidate those within its own borders who would leave the sinking ship. A May Day parade in a Communist country today is an exercise in self-parody.

In an ironic sense, Karl Marx turns out to have been right. We are witnessing on this May Day the great revolutionary drama he predicted — that epic collision of the demands of the economic order with those of the political order. The irony is that it is happening not in the free, non-Marxist West, but in the home of Marxism-Leninism, the Soviet Union itself.

Democracy and capitalism, which until a relatively few years ago had been relegated by the politically correct — here and abroad — to the ashcan of history, are triumphant throughout the world. Far from guaranteeing world socialist revolution, the U.S.S.R. stands revealed as a Third World country where fewer people probably lined up to see the weapons pass today in Red Square than lined up to get a nourishing meal at McDonald's, that wonderful American enterprise where, as the comedian Yakov Smirnoff has observed, a Soviet citizen can get something good to eat, and, even better, use what it comes wrapped in later on as toilet paper.

A little gloating on this May Day, a time when the world once cowered before Soviet might, is irresistible. But it is also an appropriate moment to consider some of the lessons we might learn from the seismic events of the last year.

One of these lessons surely is how wrong the self-defined "progressive" intellectuals of the West have been, how profoundly they misread history. Since the beginning of the Cold War, and with increasing confidence following the defeat of the U.S. in Vietnam, they have been saying that the trend in the world was toward increased state control of social, political and economic life. They have been telling us that the differences between democracy and Communism were differences of degree and not of kind, and that eventually, particularly as the Left succeeded in influencing domestic affairs of the U.S., there would be a gradual convergence between the two. The systems of capitalism and

Communism, morally equivalent in the minds of the politically correct, would meet half way.

These Leftist intellectuals have been telling us to mollify, not stand up to the Soviets. They said that the U.S.S.R. would not yield to pressure and that instead of trying to change Communism we should look to our own inner deficiencies. I think in particular back to the early Eighties when, as part of the freeze movement, American Leftist intellectuals were spreading the notion of moral equivalence with a vengeance. You remember the period when Vladimir Posner was on *Nightline*, it seemed, every week, and how he kept telling us — in a message accepted by too many Americans — that it wasn't that the Soviet Union lacked human rights but that it defined them differently than we did, and guaranteed its citizens the rights to housing, medical care, and productive work instead of free speech and all the merely "procedural" etceteras of the Bill of Rights. Different strokes for different folks, in other words.

How far off all that seems today. The U.S.S.R. has another despot, Mikhail Gorbachev, and Vladimir Posner wets a finger every morning to see which way the ideological winds are blowing. How morally imbecilic and self-doubting on our part to let such nonsense have an unchallenged public airing. Yet this fantasy of a robust and homeostatic Soviet Union was still being pursued as late as September 1984 when, as Sovietologist Richard Pipes points out in a recent issue of *Commentary* magazine, John Kenneth Galbraith, certainly a dean of Left-wing intellectualdom, if there ever was one, visited Moscow and wrote his observations in *The New Yorker* when he returned. "The Soviet economy has made great material progress in recent years," Galbraith said. "This is evident from the general urban scene...one sees it in the appearance of solid well being of the people in the streets, in the traffic, the incredible exfoliation of apartment houses and the general aspect of restaurants, theaters and shops."

As they say back in California where I come from, gag me with a spoon. These words were written a scant six months before Gorbachev took over and informed the world that the U.S.S.R. was undergoing a systemic crisis.

And this admission was just the beginning. With *glasnost* came a flood of admissions from the Soviet Union: that Stalin had indeed murdered tens of millions during his reign, something die-hards in the United States had denied. That the West was right in saying that there was no difference between Stalin and Hitler. That the invasion of Afghanistan had been offensive rather than defensive. That the esoteric radar installation at Krasnoyarsk which Leftists here at home assured us was not a threat did indeed violate the SALT treaty. In other words, that Ronald Reagan had been right when he called the U.S.S.R. an evil empire. (American Leftists would never forgive Soviet revisionists for what they had done to validate Ronald Reagan.)

There were smaller admissions as well, of course, some of them having to do with those famous "economic rights" Western progressives agreed with Vladimir Posner that the Russians had in such abundance. It turned out that it wasn't quite the upbeat place John Kenneth Galbraith had described. Actually there were a lot of homeless. A lot of those counted as having a home were actually large families occupying one or two rooms in a flat, and a lot of these homes didn't have hot running water. There was no soap in the Soviet Union, let alone meat. They didn't change sheets in Soviet hospitals, and these hospitals spread rather than combatted diseases such as AIDS by re-using syringes because of chronic shortages of everything but weapons.

No wonder when Boris Yeltsin visited this country last year he said that many of those living in our ghettos would be considered quite well off by Soviet standards.

These ongoing revelations about the poverty of Communism have provided an opportunity for the Left to admit how wrong it has been about socialism, which turns out not only to have been a mistake but also a crime. It provides an occasion for those Left-wing intellectuals who have been going over into the socialist future since Lincoln Steffens and returning to assure us that it worked, to say how wrong, how desperately and tragically wrong, they have been. But the Left has characteristically passed on this opportunity for a self inventory. Rather than seeing the crack-up of the Soviet Union for what it is — that is, as a vindication of the containment doctrine first initiated by Harry Truman and picked up and driven to a conclusion by the Reagan Administration;

rather than admitting that U.S. policy during the Cold War was correct, the self-defined progressives have talked instead about how the demise of Communism will cause a crisis in the conservative movement now that it has been deprived of the enemy. Not only that, they now suggest that there was never really a threat from Communism in the first place. It was always a fiction of our imagination, writers such as Strobe Talbott tell us. The U.S. conjured up the Cold War out of its own paranoid imaginings. The only victory we have, therefore, is illusory, nothing more than a triumph over our own psychosis.

Frankly, I do not find this sort of talk surprising. My own experience as a radical showed me years ago that Leftism was incapable of a moral balance sheet, let alone a profit and loss statement.

The Left has never learned from the tragedies it helped create. But, thank God, it is running out of countries on which to experiment. Last year, it lost the countries of Eastern Europe, countries the Right was correct in calling "captive nations" for the last forty years and the Left was wrong in calling "people's democracies" and, later, Soviet allies. More recently it has lost the foothold in Central America it worked so hard to obtain in the Eighties.

I remember the slogan of the Seventies: "Vietnam has won, Nicaragua will win." The Left thought it had established a beachhead and that the new slogan would soon be, "Nicaragua has won, El Salvador will win." That was before the vote that was held this past February in which the people of Nicaragua, finally given a voice, voted to repudiate the Sandinistas.

It must have been something to be in Managua on election night and see the Sandinista supporters in the international media crying — as it was later reported that they did — and to see Ed Asner and all the rest of the Ortega loyalists who had come for a victory celebration instead walking around looking like they'd just been told they had terminal cancer. It must have been something to see the American supporters of the Ortega regime — the Sandalistas — getting ready to pack. It has been amazing to listen to the rationales of the Left since then. Because the Left certified the elections in advance, it can't claim fraud. It has claimed, however, that American money bought Violetta Chamorro her victory. And the explanation I particularly like comes from William Sloane Coffin, who says that the Nicaraguans "voted with their bellies and not their hearts." This would make them as cynical as the American Leftists who supported those who had oppressed them for a decade.

And so there is much to reflect on this May Day — from the fall of tyrants to the abuse of history. But the best thing about May Day 1990 is that for the first time since 1917 this day can return to what it always was before the Communists seized and occupied it — a pleasant druidic ritual celebrating renewal and new life. This identity is in keeping with the death of Communism and the rebirth of freedom this past year; with the decline of oppression and the greening of the world's political landscape.

On this May Day the Left is in control only of Cuba, Albania and Berkeley, California. This is an Evil Empire we can live with. □

III

Then and Now

Chapter One

The Sixties and The Eighties

(*Peter Collier*)

First, the Sixties. Those of us for whom it was — for better or worse — the time of our lives, should have been more vigilant about who got custody of the memories. Instead we surrendered the history of the era to nostalgia merchants and socialist realists, to pop historians and radical ideologues.

These people keep assuring us that the Sixties was a time when, to turn the famous Yeats line around, the worst lacked all conviction and the best were full of passionate intensity. That it was a time when those in control of America led it cynically down the path of war and racism; a time when the nation had to be rescued by its heroic youth — those huddled idealists whose only dream was to give peace a chance. A whole generation was forced to spend itself in political activism, we are told, because of the moral iniquity of its elders.

Were there young idealists finally driven to extreme remedies in their quest for peace and justice? It was because the world they were pledged to change was one of cruelly entrenched power. Did they finally turn to violence? It was in violation of their better natures and in support of a higher law.

I don't know about the rest of you, but I'm bored by these cliches about the Sixties. There were indeed well-meaning young men and women who became involved in what we called the Movement. But they were bit players, the window dressing and cannon fodder. The Sixties as I remember it was a time of heavy hitters, freelance nihilists who became addicted to the sense of moral superiority their opposition to

---

Speech to an Accuracy in Academia Conference, Washington, D.C., June 27, 1987.

the war gave them and who used the war as justification for whatever destructive acts they chose to engage in.

Vietnam justified anointing the Black Panthers, a ghetto gang that never overcame its gangsterism, as *avant garde* and acceding to its reign of terror against moderate blacks — those "Uncle Toms" who had been trying to do something about the condition of their people long before the Panthers were discovered by radical whites, and would continue their patient work long after the Panthers had burned themselves out in violent histrionics and self-dramatization.

Vietnam justified Tom Hayden announcing to a small meeting of us radicals in Berkeley that fascism had arrived and it was time to think about beginning the civil war against "Amerika."

Vietnam justified the fifth columnism of the Weathermen, whose cadres returned from Havana in 1969 having promised the Cubans and the North Vietnamese they had met that they would begin the guerrilla struggle and would "bring the war home."

Vietnam justified everything, every excess, every insanity, every self-indulgent thought and deed.

When I think back to those times, I remember the mobs that frequently formed on the University of California campus — I was usually a part of them — and worked themselves into a frenzy before marching into Berkeley to trash the windows of the local merchants — a blow, by our tortured logic, against the petty bourgeois capitalism that supported the war against the Vietnamese. I remember so-called "activists" (we had pressured the press into using this value-free term) shouting down speakers they didn't agree with, threatening people whose views were unfashionable, and laying plans to blow up research institutes whose work they regarded, in one of those odious little phrases borrowed from the Thirties, as "objectively fascist."

Think of these images the next time someone shows you melodramatic photos of the candle-lit faces of peaceniks in tremulous vigil and says that they summarize the Sixties.

Indeed, one of the problems confronting us in the Eighties is that student radicals of the Sixties got such good press both by contemporary journals and, as time passed, by historians and social critics who ought to have known better. In fact, as a group, the activists I ran with were allergic to ideas or creative discussion. They pursued a politics of narcissism that was based on an infantile adversary posturing against the democratic values of the culture which protected them even as they sought to destroy it. Haranguing each other about "freedom" in rooms whose walls were covered by posters of Che, Mao, Lenin and other tyrants, they made cognitive dissonance into the dominant political style of the era.

One might forgive them for some of this if they had later on, as the thought and deed of the Sixties came unraveled, created a balance sheet for their acts. But this was beyond them. It would have required a maturity, not to mention a courage, which they lacked. They admitted only those "lessons" of Vietnam into the curriculum of American life that made them look good. These were not the lessons involving the Cambodian genocide and Hanoi's imperialism, as you can well imagine. They were only the lessons of American guilt and the inevitable triumph of Third World "nationalism" that we try to forestall.

The case of Fidel Castro shows the Sixties Left's inability to come to terms with its commitments. Many of us who ultimately became active in the Movement cut our political eye-teeth supporting the Cuban revolution. Just as we said at the beginning of the Sixties that we wanted to build a movement that would not follow Ike's tired and trite Americanism on the one hand, nor the Stalinism of the Old Left on the other, so Castro said that his revolution would follow neither the red, nor the red, white and blue. His would be distinct and independent — olive green. (The color of Daniel Ortega's as well.) He was a New Leftist like we were! No wonder we supported the New Society and the New Man we were sure were evolving in Cuba.

As we know now, of course, Castro was a Leninist from at least 1956, long before his tiny band of diehards came out of the Sierra Maestra. And what is he today, that fearless and independent hero we worshiped in the Sixties? An aging pimp who sells his young men to the Soviets to use in Africa in return for a huge subsidy to keep his corrupt island afloat. He has turned Cuba into a gulag, a place so horrible that 10% of its population has left since he took over, with many more ready to depart if he would let them. You would think that my old comrades would regard the fate of the Cuban revolution as a cautionary tale, a tragic development requiring a reassessment not only of Castro but of themselves. But not only do they fail to look back in anger at the way they missed the truth about Castro, but wish the same totalitarian fate on the Nicaraguans that has sunk the Cubans in a misery incomparably worse than anything they experienced under Batista and other "American puppets."

It is this Sixties tradition, unfortunately, that I see the emerging activism of the Eighties emulating. Young people ought to want to step away from the preceding generation and look at it critically as part of a process of self-definition. Instead, current "activists" have accepted the left-over radicals of the Sixties as culture heroes and gurus. Thus Abbie Hoffman, the Mortimer Snerd of the New Left, has become the Pied Piper to Amy Carter and other ingenues, an indenture that shows as well as anything else their political incompetence. Thus Tom Hayden, whom we said among ourselves twenty years ago gave opportunism a bad name, now has cachet among young campus Leftists. People like Hoffman and Hayden pour old, fermented, possibly poisonous wine into new vessels.

When I hear students at Berkeley and other campuses mouthing a saying of the official Sandinista Youth Organization, "To follow the Soviet Union is to know how to conquer, to follow the United States is to know defeat," I get a nasty case of the *deja vues*. I listen to the rallies and hear the same ignorance, the same intolerance, the same infatuation with anti-American styles and language that I heard two decades ago. It is like stepping into a time warp.

When Berkeley students chant, "No Vietnam in Central America," it is more than an admonition. It is, at a deeper level, a wish-fulfilling fantasy, the unconscious revelation of their desire for another tragic engagement between the U.S. and a plucky band of Third World nationalists that will, like fairy dust, turn the complex and ambiguous world of the Eighties into what these activists believe was the morally monochromatic world of the Sixties when there were only good guys (like Ho Chi Minh and Danny Ortega and Winnie Mandela) and bad guys (like Ollie North and the rest of us). They want to see a return to what they regard as the good old days. They want the self-indulgence people of my generation enjoyed in their own lives — the excitement and also the power. They want also another humiliating defeat for this country that will justify their hand-me-down anti-Americanism.

There are some differences between the activism of the Sixties and the Eighties, of course. The mass of today's students, for instance, are not hostile to America — not yet anyway. They realize (as indeed their radical peers do at a more cynical level) that this country's position in the world is more precarious than it was twenty-five years ago, and because it is more precarious it must be defended with more determination. The mass of students want to be integrated into America's future, rather than alienated from it. But they face a tremendous juggernaut. On the one hand there are figures outside the campuses — people like Hoffman and Hayden — telling them that they are boring and complacent and ought to get with it. More malevolently, there are also voices from within the academy urging the same message. My generation had to force its radical ideas into the university, breaking down the defenses of the faculty and the administration. Today that current of propaganda has reversed directions. The professoriate — many of them former New Leftists who in the Seventies got into tenure tracks at the very universities they had failed to burn down in the Sixties — lay their political ideas on their students, ridiculing anything they regard as conservative or patriotic, and inducting the young into the mysteries of radical scholarship, an oxymoron if I ever heard one.

In the Eighties, moreover, the university is no longer a center of authority, making a stand, however ineffectual, against ideas that are silly, dishonest or downright destructive. The university is pathologically unsure of itself, the wounds we inflicted twenty years ago never having healed. Witness all the Marxist, Peace, Gay and Women's Studies departments that have bloomed like toxic flowers in the academy of today. The university does not tell students — as it tried to do in the Sixties, before caving in — about standards and values. It is a fearful, emasculated institution filled with double talk and double standards.

Now my generation had its faults, but lack of candor was not one of them. We said that we were radicals, insurrectionists, revolutionaries. We were frank about what we had in mind, as our slogans showed — *Up Against the Wall, Bring the War Home, Tear the Mother Down.*

Eighties radicals, by contrast, like the role of the wolf in sheep's clothing. They have adopted the popular frontism of the Thirties. Instead of admitting who and what they are — a force out to destroy American power — they posture as sincere liberals who are only in favor of peace and justice. They do this even as they work for totalitarian solutions, in the manner of their newly canonized martyr Benjamin Linder (killed by Nicaraguan peasants who liked neither the Sandinista *comandantes*, nor their Sandalista friends).

This is, to say the least, an alarming tendency. Alarming too are the popular fronts today's "activists" work through. I have in mind an organization like CISPES, the Committee in Solidarity with the People of El Salvador. This organization has chapters on campuses across the country. Student radicals either don't know that CISPES was formed in 1979 by an El Salvadoran Marxist guerrilla agent working with Cuban intelligence, or they don't care. Perhaps they don't know and wouldn't care if they did. But this is the kind of Left that they seem to like — one that works through apparently "objective" fronts which actually are intelligence organizations set up by America's enemies.

So, it looks as though we are on the threshold of a Leftism that is like that of the Sixties in its romanticized affection for totalitarian movements like the Sandinistas, the FMLN in El Salvador, and the African National Congress in South Africa. And like the Left of the Thirties, it is its intention to work through deceitfully layered organizational arrangements.

The worst of the Sixties and the worst of the Thirties — that's a combination to be wary of. □

Chapter Two

Student Activists: Then and Now

(David Horowitz)

What does Marxism have to offer the bourgeois university? Preferably nothing. That is, Marxism can do nothing *for* the university; the real question is what can Marxists do *to* and *in* the university?"
— *Harvard Professor Richard Lewontin*

On April 15, 1980, as invading Soviet armies poured across the Afghanistan border, a thousand students assembled for a "'Stop the War' Teach-In" on the University of California campus at Berkeley. Their protests were not addressed to the Soviet invader, however, but to the Carter White House which had condemned the attack and requested defense increases and a military draft as deterrents to Soviet aggression. Speaker after speaker rose to denounce these measures as manifestations of a resurgent American militarism and anti-Communist paranoia and to condemn them as preludes to "another Vietnam" and threats to the peace.

These echoes of the radical past were far from incidental at the event which served to kick off the activism of a new political decade. Those in the crowd who were too young to make the allusions for themselves were guided by the parade of middle-aged political veterans who mounted the rostrum at the invitation of the protest organizers. Communist Party leader Angela Davis and Berkeley radical Congressman Ron Dellums may have played peripheral roles in the Sixties political drama, but they were center-stage at its Eighties revival. Recalling how similar "teach-ins" and anti-draft protests had changed history in Vietnam, they applauded the symbolism the organizers had contrived: the

Speech to an Accuracy in Academia Conference, Washington, D.C., June 27, 1987.

time had come, they said, to revive the political enthusiasms of the past and its radical discontents.

If the episode revealed the self-conscious effort of Eighties activism to identify itself as a child of the Sixties, it also exposed the contradiction inherent in such a claim. For the radicalism of the Sixties had identified itself as a child *without* political parents. Its most famous slogan — You Can't Trust Anyone Over Thirty — meant exactly what it said.

Sixties activism was born as a self-conscious attempt to reject one tainted politics (Stalinism) and to atone for another ("cold war liberalism.") Therein lay its redeeming originality and its aura of idealism and political innocence. Eighties activism was born in an opposite effort to *revive* the tainted politics that had been previously rejected and to appropriate the aura of idealism and innocence that the rejection had produced. Therein lies the cynicism of its political commitments and the deviousness of its political styles.

The cynicism of today's radicals is immediately apparent in their self-presentation as "progressives" and "liberals." Eighties radicals are not only comfortable with these political labels, they insist on them, denouncing as "McCarthyite" efforts to penetrate their deceptive surfaces. But, as an ancient wisdom shrewdly observes, all political justice begins with a clarity about names.

The radicals who laid siege to the "System" in the Sixties and today's activists are, in fact, successive generations of an American Left which is itself a branch of an international Marxism whose roots lie in the solidarities of the Soviet Revolution of 1917. It is a Left which, having been shattered by the traumas that followed Stalin's death, embarked as the Sixties began on a long and painful process of rebirth.

Sixties radicals situated themselves squarely within this tradition by identifying themselves as a "New Left" — a term which had been adopted by Communists all over the world who had decided to repudiate Stalin's crimes, but not the cause that had led to them. By calling themselves a "New Left," they declared their intention to distance themselves from the pro-Soviet Left of their parents' generation, but also to pick up its ideological pieces — to begin politically where their parents had left off. On the one hand this meant a renewal of faith in their Old Left ideals. On the other it meant the adoption of a political style that was truly new.

Since they had rejected the Old Left's loyalties to the Soviet Union (which had to be concealed), the New Leftists had no need to disguise their agendas or to pose as progressives as their predecessors had done. They could be radical and proud. They had no desire to infiltrate liberal institutions in order to shape and influence the democratic process: their intention was to make "a revolution in the streets."

As the Sixties began, these New Leftists were joined by another group of political orphans, the offspring of their parents' liberal antagonists, whose anti-Communist crusade had incurred a debilitating taint in the McCarthy excess. At the outset of the Sixties, the two groups joined forces on one side of a conflict that would define their relationship to the political past and determine the course of their political future.

The scene of the conflict was SDS, which was to become the pre-eminent organization of Sixties radicalism. SDS had begun the decade as the student arm of the Socialist Party, an anti-Communist faction of the Left. The conflict was over the radicals' determination to include Communists in their political ranks and their rejection of "anti-Communism" as a political principle. This caused a break between the SDS young turks and the over-thirty veterans of SDS' parent organization. Thus, the rejection of anti-Communism was the self-evident truth with which the New Left declared its independence at the outset of its radical career.

The New Left's earlier rejection of the scourges associated with Stalin and McCarthy at first fostered an ethos — non-violent, democratic, idealistic, "American" — that allowed radicals to join the civil rights movement in its early triumphs. But deep in their political hearts the radicals regarded these triumphs as worrisome subversions of their real agendas. The democratic passions and non-violent tactics they had temporarily embraced were obstacles to political agendas that could never be satisfied by peaceful means or mere reforms.

By mid-decade, America was engaged in a war against Communist aggression in South Vietnam whose tribulations provided the radicals with the rationale they needed to discard the liberal ideals, that made them uncomfortable, and to return to their political roots. By the end of the decade the radicals had relinquished any commitment they might have had to the purposes and values of American democracy. Proclaiming themselves Marxists and Leninists and at war with "Amerika," the radicals embraced America's totalitarian enemies and revived the Communist loyalties of the past. With these twin betrayals of country and self, the New Left's ten-year effort to make a "revolution in the streets" ended in defeat.

As in a previous era, a radical politics had discredited itself and died. But, as before, the radical faith survived. During the Seventies, radicals began a "long march through the institutions" of the American mainstream. While liberals wrestled with their guilts over America's anti-Communist war in Vietnam, Leftists struggled to come to terms with the Communist heritage they had previously rejected. While liberal sentiment congealed in the recriminations of a political divorce, the community of the Left was enveloped in the nostalgia of a political reunion. In a cultural outpouring which included films like *The Front* and books like *The Romance of American Communism*, Leftists attempted to rehabilitate the discredited forbears whose politics they once had rejected and to celebrate the old reds whose corrupt and divided loyalties they once had scorned.

It is this reunion that has given birth to the Left we see before us.

The Sixties Left had no political teachers, but it did have a political guide: the memory of the crimes and treasons its predecessors had justified in the Revolution's name. The Eighties Left has no such guide, but it has plenty of teachers in the hardcore survivors of the Sixties who betrayed their own political ideals and embraced a discredited past. The teachers of today's Left are the political diehards whose radicalism is defined in solidarities with Communist totalitarianism and an anti-Americanism immune to the lessons of its own experience. The most dramatic civil rights revolution in the history of any 20th century nation, the most spectacular display of democratic process in a self-inflicted defeat in Vietnam, the most expansive demonstration of political tolerance in a postwar amnesty for America's "enemies within" — all served merely to harden the hatred for America that these radicals felt.

In sum, the Eighties Left did not originate, like its predecessor, in a rejection of Communist politics and Soviet empire, or in renewed appreciation for American democracy. Under the malign tutelage of its political elders, the Eighties Left began in apologies for Soviet aggression in Afghanistan, refusals to condemn Communist oppression in Vietnam, solidarities with Communist revolutions in Central America, and denunciations of America's democracy as racist and militarist, and a threat to the peace.

Where the New Left had begun with traumatic lessons in the nightmare realities of Marxist liberations and had rejected the Old Left's subversive loyalties to Marxist regimes, the Eighties Left was the beneficiary of no such guides. In the political school of *its* radical teachers, the lessons it learned about Vietnam contained no instruction in the brutal consequences of Communist victories, or the imperialist expansions of Communist empires, or the costly human toll of American defeats.

It has been more than a decade since American armies have been at war in Vietnam or anywhere else. But while America has remained militarily passive, the Communist victors have been on the march. In Indochina, Hanoi's armies have blazed a trail of military conquest and colonial occupation; in Africa, Cuban expeditionary forces have spread famine and bloodshed and Communist oppression; and in Afghanistan, Soviet marauders have torched a nation and made refugees of half a population in one of the most savage invasions of modern times. But, from its inception, the Eighties Left has been deaf and blind to these events. Through all these years of Communist conquest and of human suffering caused by socialist regimes, the United States has remained the only real enemy of American radicals.

In the radicals' school, the lesson of Vietnam is just this: America is the enemy; America can be defeated. *Vietnam Has Won, El Salvador Will Win*. All that is necessary is a Communist guerrilla army backed by the Soviets on the field of battle, and a political force in solidarity with the Communists inside the United States.

The solidarity Left of the Eighties begins where the Sixties left off: in a politics of secession from America's democracy and service to the totalitarian cause. Because its politics is Marxist, it is a continuation of a war begun in 1917 by other means. Because its politics is war by other means, there is no room for candor in its rhetoric or integrity in its agendas. These pay lip service to humane goals and liberal values in order to manipulate democratic publics. But liberality and humanity are not the real commitments of the American Left. Its real commitments are to future American defeats and to Communist victories like Vietnam.

The strategy of today's radicals is a strategy invented by the old Communist Left in its heyday as a fifth column for Joseph Stalin. It is a strategy that forms "progressive" coalitions for "Peace and Justice in Central America" in order to further its real goals which are a Marxist police state in Nicaragua and a Communist victory in neighboring El Salvador. The Eighties Left invokes democratic principles and America's interests only to promote its covert agendas which are anti-American and anti-democratic. That is why it is eager to deny democratic rights to its political opponents, whenever the opportunity appears. The radical Left is a fascist force with a human face, the carrier of an ideological virus as deadly as AIDS. Uncontained, it will first subvert and eventually destroy the immune system of the body politic.

What can be done to strengthen democracy's defenses against this attack? The Sixties provide a relevant lesson. The Sixties Left was numerically small and politically weak. Not a single one of its political achievements would have been possible through its own efforts alone. Its successes were made possible by a factor beyond its control: the collapse of the liberal center of American politics, the surrender of the establishment to which it had laid siege.

Crippled by guilt over Vietnam the liberal center lost the will to defend itself and its traditional values, and thus conferred legitimacy on the radicals and their political agendas. Instead of maintaining the radicals' isolation, the liberal establishment gave them access to the very institutions — the media, the universities and the Democratic Party — that they had so diligently attempted to destroy.

* * *

Today the legacy of this political masochism is everywhere evident, above all in academic institutions. Radicals who violate the canons of intellectual discipline and the principles of academic freedom are not promptly expelled from the community they despise. Instead their political savagery and contempt for academic values are treated as expressions of an idealistic concern that the academy ought to heed and respect. Administrators at Columbia University have even devised a specially lenient disciplinary code for students whose offenses occur in the course of political protests. In this way, an institution which was brought to its knees by radicals in the Sixties encourages the destructive agendas of their political heirs as an integral part of the educational process. The short-term result is that every spring Columbia radicals find a pretext to lay siege to the university and bring its functions to a halt. A year ago the occasion was the radicals' desire to inflame a racial conflict in southern Africa, this year to ignite a race war at home. The longer-term result is that the radicals' agendas are accepted as legitimate by the very communities they seek to destroy. By failing to enforce its principles and standards, the academic community not only strengthens its radical enemies, but weakens its own foundations and accelerates its decline.

In the last two decades in America there has indeed been a precipitous decline in academic standards and scholarship. In classrooms across the country ideological indoctrination has supplanted intellectual inquiry as academic discipline. Marxism, long consigned with flat earthism to the intellectual mausoleum, has been raised from the dead to a place of respect in the university curriculum. Racial and gender discrimination (against Asians and white males) has been institutionalized as enlightened academic policy. Professional associations once devoted to the promotion of scholarship have been turned into political lobbies for totalitarian causes and terrorist elites.

The problem that faces the university community is the problem that faces the democracy itself. A community that refuses to recognize its enemies is a community that is unable to defend itself, that has lost its will to survive. The continuing failure of the liberal center to withdraw the cloak of legitimacy from the illiberal shoulders of the hate-America Left, is a reflection of the continuing failure of liberal nerve that began with Vietnam. Its root cause is a loss of faith in the liberal values of

American society and in the role that American power must play in the fate of liberal hopes in the world at large. It is only when liberal America is once again able to believe in itself that it will be able to recognize its radical enemies and to join with American conservatives who are the contemporary defenders of traditional liberal values, and who have begun to wage the battles that must be won if America's democracy is to survive. □

Chapter Three

Angela Davis and Me

(David Horowitz)

Imagine that a group of Dartmouth students had invited a Grand Dragon of the Ku Klux Klan to speak at Dartmouth; that the Grand Dragon agreed to come to Dartmouth for a $10,000 honorarium; that having come, he had launched into a semi-literate diatribe against women, blacks, and American democracy. Let us suppose, further, that four Dartmouth fraternity presidents were in the audience and had stood up to cheer when the Grand Dragon was done.

A similar event actually took place at this campus — except that it was the Dartmouth Administration and four College deans who played host and cheerleaders to the racist demagogue; that she was not only invited, but invited to keynote a major College commemoration; that she was introduced by a college dean as an "example" of a "committed black woman activist [who] has chosen to make a difference;" that her targets were men, whites, Jews, and President Bush, instead of the suspects mentioned, and that the hate groups she represented play a far more sinister role in America's political life and are implicated in far greater evils globally than the pathetic remnants of the Ku Klux Klan. I am speaking, I need hardly explain, of comrade Angela Davis and the Communist Party, and an event that took place only a month ago.

* * *

Angela Davis and Communism are institutions that I know something about. Both my parents were card-carrying members of the American Communist Party, whose Central Committee Ms. Davis now graces. She and I belong to the same political generation. I helped to found the New Left in the early Sixties, at the time she was joining the

---

Speech given at Dartmouth College, November 17, 1988.

Communist International. A decade later, I helped to create a community base for the Black Panther Party in the East Oakland ghetto. It was a time when she was helping Black Panther Field Marshal George Jackson — then an inmate at San Quentin prison in San Francisco — to amass an arsenal for his private liberation army. Equipped with the weapons Angela Davis provided, this army murdered half a dozen people in Marin County, California in the years 1970 and 1971. I would like to take a moment, therefore, to share with you some insights into the perverse mind of the individual whom your president has seen fit to support so generously with your college tuition, under the rationale of providing for your educational enrichment.

In 1956, when I was 17 years old, the Israeli secret service, The Mossad, smuggled Nikita Khrushchev's secret speech about Stalin's crimes out of the Kremlin, and delivered it to the Central Intelligence Agency and the *New York Times* which printed the text in full. Only today, thirty years later (thanks to *glasnost*), can citizens of the Soviet Union also read what their late leader, Nikita Khrushchev, said at that time. In the West, the significance of the Khruhschev report lay not in its revelation of Soviet crimes — about which the world was already informed — but in the fact that the Communist pope had finally confirmed what conservative anti-Communists like William F. Buckley had been saying for two decades and more. And what Communists and fellow-traveling Leftists as well as liberal "progressives" had been denying and denouncing as red-baiting lies for all of that time.

It is important to remember what the socialist crimes of the Stalin era actually were: mass murders on a scale that exceeded those of Adolf Hitler. Tens of millions of people deliberately starved and brutally slaughtered; tens of millions more incarcerated in the infamous gulag archipelago — a network of concentration camps whose conditions rivaled Maidenek and Auschwitz.

During the slaughters conducted by the Stalinist police state, the American Communist Party supplied political gofers and cheerleaders for the slaughterers. The American Communist Party — in whose community I grew to adulthood — always pretended to outsiders that it was just a band of "progressive" activists who wanted to "make a difference"; but, in reality, it was a conspiratorial fifth column, operating within America's borders on behalf of the Soviet mass murderers outside. For its Soviet masters, the American Communist Party provided willing intellectuals like Lillian Hellman to act as propagandists, to smear and discredit all those who attempted to tell the truth about the Soviet atrocities, libeling them with accusations that would have put a witch-hunter like McCarthy to shame; it provided spies, like Julius and Ethel Rosenberg, to steal the secrets of America's atomic weapons; it infiltrated the Democratic Party and the top-most reaches of the American government with agents like Harry Dexter White and Alger Hiss, to further Moscow's imperial cause.

But when Khrushchev's speech appeared in the *New York Times* in February 1956, admitting the terrible crimes that socialism had committed, the faithful were shocked; and then demoralized. The Communist movement began to disintegrate. In Hungary, dissidents rebelled against the Stalinist nightmare and Soviet tanks rolled across the border to crush them. In America, there were dissidents, too, who spoke out in support of the Hungarian freedom fighters. They were led by Spanish Civil War veteran John Gates, who wrote an editorial in the Communist *Daily Worker* denouncing the unconscionable Soviet act. But these voices also were crushed.

When John Gates and his supporters were silenced by their own party, they decided there was no honorable course but to leave its ranks. So morally bankrupt had Communism become that any Communist with a shred of integrity left at that time. The party which had numbered 60,000 shrank overnight to a mere 6,000. Those who stayed were the Stalinist diehards — morally comatose, political sycophants, unswerving in their loyalty to the Soviet state. The leading toady among them was the party's "theoretician" Herbert Aptheker. While his comrades expressed their outrage at the Soviet betrayal of their socialist ideals, Herbert Aptheker sat down to write a tract called *The Truth About Hungary,* defending the Soviet tanks which flattened Budapest by libeling the Hungarian freedom fighters as "fascists" and "Nazis," and repeating every lie of the Kremlin line.

When I was sixteen, just before these events took place, Herbert Aptheker was my teacher at a Communist school of Marxism in New York. A few years later, as the events were unfolding, Angela Davis began her own political career in the Aptheker household, co-founding a Communist youth front called "Advance," with Aptheker's daughter, and her best Communist friend.

Although, I, too, had been part of the Communist youth movement, I did not follow the path that took Angela Davis into the party in its most politically corrupt and degenerate hour. Instead, along with many other Communist offspring of my generation I helped to found a "New Left." Through this New Left we hoped to rescue socialism from the clutches of the mass murderers and their "progressive" accomplices, to make sure that such crimes would not happen again. During the Sixties, we New Leftists despised young Communists, like Angela Davis, and the old Stalinist hacks who had stayed in the party, and kept them at arm's length. We would not have invited them — let alone bribed them — to speak on our platforms, as Dartmouth's president has recently done.

But, in the end, we New Leftists failed in our efforts to create a radical movement that had moral integrity and political independence, that was not in league with totalitarian regimes. As the Sixties ended, the New Left was once again becoming a fifth column for Communist powers, supporting new crimes in the name of "solidarity" with socialist police states. The New Left fell in love with Communist tyrants like Mao Zedong, whose Great Leaps took the lives of more than 25 million people, and Fidel Castro, whose Communist legions have propped up dictators in Angola and Ethiopia, spreading death and famine among millions more.

It was at the end of the Sixties, too, that Angela Davis became the lover and political comrade of George Jackson, a maximum security inmate in San Quentin prison, who was awaiting trial for pre-meditated murder. At the time, Angela Davis and other Leftists — including myself — defended George Jackson as an innocent black victim of racist "Amerika." But to intimates on his own defense committee, George Jackson boasted that he was guilty as charged, and had killed twelve other men in prison besides. One of his revolutionary schemes was to poison the water system of Chicago, which was the city where he had grown up.

Jackson was awaiting trial for the murder of prison guard John Mills. Mills had been killed in retaliation for the shooting death of a black convict during a prison fracas. Neither Jackson nor anyone else ever claimed that John Mills had anything to do with the previous shooting. Jackson murdered John Mills simply because he was white.

On August 7, 1970, shortly before George Jackson was scheduled to go on trial, his seventeen-year-old brother Jonathan, carrying weapons owned by Angela Davis, entered a Marin County courtroom and kidnapped a judge, an assistant district attorney and a Marin County juror. The young Jackson intended to use the hostages to set his brother free. The attempt failed. The judge, Jonathan and two other prisoners were killed and Angela Davis disappeared from sight. When she was finally caught, she was indicted as an accomplice to murder, but the prosecution was unable to prove that she had given Jackson the weapons or knew his intentions in advance. Many radicals familiar with the Black Panthers and the Communist Party, and with the relationship between Angela Davis and the prisoner George Jackson, drew conclusions of their own.

A year later, George Jackson attempted to escape from San Quentin. One guard was shot to death and three others were tied up by Jackson and his comrades, who slit their throats with razors. Jackson was killed. At his funeral, Angela Davis praised Jackson for dying a hero's death and reaffirmed his declaration of war against the "racist" society that had allegedly "killed him." But Jackson's death did not end the trail of those tragic events.

Before his escape attempt, Jackson had been defended and made internationally famous through the efforts of a Jewish radical attorney named Fay Stender, who was a political ally and friend of Angela Davis. When Jackson asked Fay Stender to provide him with a weapon to launch his escape, she refused. In 1979, she was punished for this "betrayal" by a member of Jackson's prison gang who appeared at her door in the middle of the night and shot her five times at point blank range. A year later, paralyzed and condemned to a lifetime of pain, Fay Stender committed suicide. Fay Stender had devoted her entire life to radical and feminist causes and to the defense of Huey Newton, George Jackson and hundreds of other black men in prison whom she felt were oppressed. But Angela Davis did not come to her funeral, or speak a word in her praise.

One of George Jackson's prison gangsters — a rapist and thug named Fleeta Drumgo — was an accomplice in the assault on Fay Stender. Fleeta Drumgo had helped Jackson murder John Mills, but was later released on parole. A drug addict, he attempted to sell information about Fay Stender's assailants to other Leftists concerned about her fate. Soon after, he was killed in a gang-style execution. Angela Davis did speak at Fleeta Drumgo's funeral and eulogized him as a "Communist martyr."

The Communist and pro-Communist Left for whom Angela Davis is a hero and leader is a fanatic, nihilistic, and — given the opportunity — violent party. I do not exaggerate in saying that I put my life in a measure of danger just to say what I have said here. The diehards of the Left are ideological hate-mongers, more dangerous today because they have the protective goodwill and support of institutions such as Dartmouth. And not only Dartmouth but college faculties across this nation, where Communists and political Marxists and fellow-travelers of the totalitarian fifth column have already gained an alarming foothold.

* * *

Is it an accident that Marxists and Communists should be involved in political murder and mass murder from California to Cambodia and from Ethiopia to Afghanistan? Or that Communist revolutions should result in nation-size prison camps from Managua to Warsaw and from Havana to Hanoi? After seventy years of bloody history, the answer is obvious. It is no more an accident that Marxist doctrines of class hatred should have led to the gulag than that Nazi doctrines of race hatred should have led to Maidenek and Auschwitz.

Both Nazism and Marxism are doctrines rooted in the messianic ambitions and gnostic illusions that the enlightenment unleashed; both evoke the salvationist claims of the socialist promise; both are apocalyptic visions, proposing final solutions to what have been timeless problems of the human condition.

Both Nazism and Marxism set out to create the socialist future by first destroying the bourgeois, democratic present and erecting their utopias on its smoldering ruins. Both intended to restore the lost unity of mankind by first dividing humanity into opposing camps — us and them — the children of light and the carriers of darkness, those who are saved and those who are damned. National Socialism proposed to build its utopia on a foundation of race — the creation of a genetically purified Aryan breed; international socialism proposes to build its utopia on the basis of class — the creation of a morally purified, proletarian strain: the new Soviet man and woman. Both have murdered millions, creating no new utopias but rather new social hells that have caused human suffering on unprecedented scales.

The founding prophet of the Leftist faith, Karl Marx, was a deracinated Jew, whose father had changed his name from Herschel to Heinrich and converted to Christianity to advance his career. The young Marx grew into a man consumed by hatred for his own community and the communities around him. Internalizing the worst anti-Semitic stereotypes, he incorporated them into his early revolutionary vision, identifying Jews as symbols of the system of private property and bourgeois democracy he wanted to destroy: "The god of the Jews has been secularized and has become the god of this world," Marx wrote. "Money is the jealous God of Israel, beside which no other God may stand." Once the revolution succeeded in "destroying the empirical essence of Judaism," he promised, "the Jew will become impossible." This early Marxist formulation is the transparent seed of the mature vision, causing the writer Paul Johnson to characterize Marxism as "the anti-Semitism of the intellectuals."

The international Communist creed that Marx invented is a creed of hate and self-hate. The solution that Marx proposed to the Jewish "problem" was to eliminate the system that "creates" the Jew. The Jews, he said, are only symptoms of a more extensive evil that must be eradicated: capitalism. The Jews are only symbols of a more pervasive enemy that must be destroyed: capitalists. In the politics of the Left, racist hatred is directed not only against Jewish capitalists but against all capitalists; not only against capitalists, but against anyone who is not poor, and who is white; and ultimately against Western civilization itself. The Marxist revolution is anti-Semitism elevated to a global principle.

The university in America is now a battle ground between those who value the freedoms we have developed in this country over two hundred years and the totalitarians of the Left who have been battling for the last seventy to take them away. It is the responsibility of those who cherish free institutions and the culture that sustains them to stand up against the barbarians who are already within the gates. □

Chapter Four

Racial Consciousness

(Peter Collier)

Can we build a color blind society? A noble dream, which is the essence of Martin Luther King's call for a world in which a man is judged by the content of his character rather than the color of his skin. But an impossible dream, it seems to me, given the world we now live in. Frankly, I think that the question should rather be, "Can we keep our culture and institutions from being defaced by officially sanctioned color consciousness?" Can we keep racial division and ethnic animosity from being permanently injected into our public discourse and our private lives?

It is ridiculous that it should come to this, given the distance we have traveled as a nation. But has any country ever voluntarily poured so much money and effort into recognizing its guilty past and trying to remedy the plight of its least fortunate? We have seen a revolution in our own lifetime. Twenty-five years ago, when I went South during the civil rights movement, I saw schools, buses, and public accommodations which were racially segregated not only by law, but by customs that seemed far more durable and unyielding. I thought this situation would change, but only by the slow geologic processes of time or perhaps after the bloody race war that apocalypticians of the Sixties predicted. But it happened overnight — an unprecedented revolution in institutions and in manners as well — and it happened virtually bloodlessly. Yes, there are skinheads out there, there is a KKK and also a David Duke, but these are marginal phenomena now, at least for the time being, however much some on the Left would like them to function as the scab which, when picked, will bleed the racial strife which proves America's irredeemable evil.

Speech to a panel, titled Can We Build a Color Blind Society?, *at a Conservative Leadership Conference, December 1, 1989.*

Nor is it true that race is for us, like sex was for the Victorians, the dirty little secret swept under the rug and stuffed into the closet. Far from being on the periphery of our vision, blacks and black consciousness are at the center of popular culture. Oprah, Cosby, Michael Jackson, Mike Tyson, Eddie Murphy — these are not just entertainers, they are multi-million dollar conglomerates, among the most powerful figures in our society. I remember when I was younger it was said that the National Basketball Association dare not let more than half its players be black because revenues would plummet disastrously. Today sellout crowds which are more than 80% white pay upwards of twenty dollars a seat to watch teams which are more than 80% black.

Far from stagnating, the racial situation in this country has witnessed change which must be regarded as phenomenal. Consider the facts and figures. Between 1977-82, black-owned businesses grew by over 50% to 340,000, which grossed over $12 billion. In 1940 the typical black earned 43% of the typical white; 40 years later it was 73%. In 1940, 8% of blacks had incomes higher than the white average; in 1980, 29% did. And in the last ten years these figures have continued to improve as the black middle class continues to expand and to narrow the gap with its white counterparts.

In 1964, when I was in Alabama, there were fewer than 300 black elected officials. Today there are more than 5,000, including most of the mayors of our largest cities. Douglas Wilder was recently elected governor of Virginia. Of course those who are obsessed by the guilt of Americans find a worm even in this apple, pointing out that fewer people actually voted for Wilder than said they did in exit polls. What is the more significant fact, that a few people lied or that a black was elected with massive white backing in the cornerstone state of the confederacy? Do these little white lies told at the exit poll indicate racism or a fear, in the present coercive atmosphere, of being called a racist for not voting for a black even if the voter thought he was not the best man? This epilogue to the election has transformed from a glass which is all the way full into one which is half empty.

We have made tremendous progress, but it seems that the better we do as a society, the more desperate some are to prove that our condign heart as a nation is white with racism. Thus the novelist Toni Morrison, whose books have won prizes and large advances and, in a truly depressing instance of affirmative action, have even been placed next to the works of Aristotle and Proust in the damaged curriculum of Western civilization at Stanford and other universities, indicts this country and says that in no part of her life has she "felt like an American." And that noted social philosopher Spike Lee recently stated, in a comment immediately quoted by the media with the awe accorded to an aphorism by George Bernard Shaw, "In America to be black is good enough reason to be killed." Yes, this is true, but killed not by some mad dog white created by the youthful and pampered filmmaker's imagination, but by another real life black. For 98% of blacks who are killed — and murder *is* the leading cause of death for young black males Spike Lee's age — are killed by other blacks. None of the writers who cited Lee's statement so respectfully pointed this out, just as nobody makes a point of the fact that in 1985, according to data recently cited by Pat Buchanan, of 625,000 incidents of interracial violence, nine out of ten were black against white.

The fact is that as the law *has* become color blind and the government more generous, as whites have become more enlightened — at this moment of maximum change in the tilt of the playing field, charges of racism multiply on the part of privileged black intellectuals who do the wrong thing, and we find that the civil rights establishment — this is what it is, an establishment, not a movement — insists that equality of opportunity be superseded by an enforced equality of outcome.

We have entered the era of the double standard, which colorizes our society rather than making it color blind. The tongue-tied banalities of an Al Campanis or Jimmy the Greek are taken as symptomatic of something deeper, while the vicious ravings of Louis Farrakhan, part of an anti-Semitism that has become a virulent strain in black intellectual life, are not. In a recent essay in the *National Review,* John O'Connor captured the essence of the double standard by simply citing the headlines by which the New York *Times* announced a pair of recent events. One was, "Youths Rape and Beat Central Park Jogger." The other was, "Black Youth is Killed in Brooklyn by Whites in Attack Called Racist."

The double standard is in control of our system of higher education and threatens its integrity and survival. I recently talked to an admissions officer at the University of California, where I went as a student and have since taught at, on occasion, as a visiting writer. He revealed that the average SAT scores of blacks admitted in this year's freshman class were around 925, about 400 points lower than the score of white and Asian students. It does these students no favor to admit them. Nearly 70% will fail to graduate, according to past statistics kept but not publicized by the university. It is an act of cynicism and cowardice on the part of an administration, convinced that it is racism not to have a yearly quota of black faces, to admit these students. But rather than refraining from these gestures of affirmative racism, the UC administration proceeds to create what it regards as a congenial atmosphere for them. This involves capitulating to the Left, which sees minority students as a Trojan horse for its assault on Western values and democratic institutions. Thus the university promulgates laws against free speech lest someone say something insensitive. It de-canonizes the curriculum which consists of too many books written by DWEMs — Dead White European Males. And it begins to make race a factor in the hiring of new faculty — race, not merit or ability. Some of the guidelines given to hiring committees in various departments make about as much sense as ordering the Boston Celtics to choose a 5'2" Asian power forward as their first draft pick every year.

The university does all this and then professes to be surprised and alarmed by the fact that there is racial tension on campus. How could it be otherwise? Could one devise a system better designed to create racial hostility if one tried? Could there be a system more calculated to make blacks and other groups, benefitting from the double standard, feel embattled and whites and Asians, victimized by it, feel ripped off?

I have said that blacks are used to advance a Left-wing agenda in the university. I could go further and say that the civil rights movement, such as it is, is a Left-wing movement. The Black Caucus is a Left Caucus. The leading black spokesman, Jesse Jackson, is an only partially reconstructed New Leftist. Black leaders have enforced a reign of terror over black intellectuals who beg to differ from the racial orthodoxy they have set up. This is true not just of black conservatives like Thomas Sowell or black libertarians like Glenn Loury, but also of individuals like

Shelby Steele, author of the prize-winning *Content of Our Character*, who outraged the black establishment by seeking explanations for the racial dilemma in the psychology of victimhood rather than in the dogmatic assertion of racism.

The Left is not interested in solutions for problems generally: its power comes from malaise. The black Left is not interested in a solution for our racial problems; it is interested in rhetoric and gesture, but not solutions. Back in 1965 Daniel Patrick Moynihan foresaw what has become the most desperate social crisis of our time, the emergence of a black underclass whose existence was made possible by the distintegration of the black family. As Glenn Loury and others have shown, Moynihan's research had convinced Lyndon Johnson to make remedying this problem a focus of his civil rights philosophy. But then black Leftists in the civil rights establishment, with their "blame the victim" guilt-trip, side-tracked this approach. They instead insisted, in apocalyptic rhetoric characteristic of the time — rhetoric designed to destroy rather than create — on "alternative solutions" such as a $100 million Freedom Budget. As these leaders indicted the capitalist system which then, like now, is the best hope for the black community, President Johnson was turned off, and a historic opportunity was missed.

We see the consequences of this missed opportunity today in a black underclass living in a squalor that would have made Dickens blush. This poverty is perdurable; it is isolated and self re-creating. It is "feminized." In the late 1950s, 30% of poor black families were headed by women; today it is more than 60%. In 1959, only 15% of black births were out of wedlock. Today, over 90% of the babies born to black teenagers are illegitimate. Teenaged mothers, grandmothers in their late twenties, great-grandmothers in their early forties: this is the family structure of the underclass. For these women, the government has become the spouse of first and last resort. They are married to welfare just as the men of the underclass are married to drugs and violence. They are without the things commonly thought to define humanity: family, work, obedience to law, transmission of life-sustaining values from one generation to the next.

We are lectured over and over again by the Left-wing mentality that controls the racial agenda that this is a white problem. That this problem exists because of white neglect, because of white history. That it is the result of 400 years of slavery. This is absurd, a calumny against the black people who have already pulled themselves out of the ghetto and also against those who would, if given half a chance. As the eminent black sociologist William Julius Wilson has pointed out, in 1940 only 17% of black families were headed by women and most of them by women who were widows, not abandoned. Seventeen percent in 1940 and 70 percent today: how could the heritage of slavery have gotten so much more oppressive as we have gotten fifty years farther away from it?

To say what is true — that the problem of the black ghetto is predominantly a black problem, predominantly a crisis of values and behavior— is to be accused of racism, of "blaming the victim." But it is true nonetheless. For generations of Americans, poverty was real but transient, something that could be overcome by hard work and long-term effort. This has been the experience of our most recent immigrants — Cambodians and Vietnamese — as well. But Sixties contempt for work and nonsense about being forced into "dead-end jobs" (as if there were such a thing) have wreaked havoc on the underclass. For the rest of America, these ideas are fatuous cliches fit only for *New Yorker* cartoons; for the black community they have become parasitic rationales for further descent to the lower depths.

The Left used to say that the black world was a colony inside the mother country. That was absurd enough. But today, because of the Left's solutions, there is something even worse: a Third World scene of devastation inside an accessible First World of plenty. How do black intellectuals and taste-makers respond to the problem? Listen to black singer Tracy Chapman in *Material World*:

> Call it upward mobility
> But you've been sold down the river
> Just another form of slavery
> And the whole man-made white world
> As your master.

If it was just the adolescent whine of a young singer it would be one thing, but the same fiction is spread throughout the black community by supposedly responsible adults. Tune out, drop out, become a victim.

So, to come back to the topic. Can we build a colorblind society? I would have to say no. Not while we have an underclass beaten so black and blue by demagogues posing as their saviors. Not while we have double standards and preferences. Not while "racism" is asserted as a catch-all explanation for every difficulty black people face. Not while we have Leftists — black and white together — cynically manipulating the race issue and using it to indict America rather than bring all black people fully into a system which promises them their last best hope. We had a phrase for people like this in the Sixties: they are part of the problem, not part of the solution. ◻

Chapter Five

The New Racism and the Radical Left

(David Horowitz)

At the height of the civil rights revolution of the Sixties, a group of black radicals led by James Farmer rejected Lyndon Johnson's offer to participate in "the Great Society" and demanded instead $400 million in reparations for the 400 years of slavery that African Americans had suffered in this country. Years later, the black economist Thomas Sowell countered this argument by citing the gains that black Americans had made since their arrival from Africa and comparing their current status and economic condition with the terrible plight of their countrymen who had been left behind. Without attempting to diminish the horrors of slavery or of the crime that had brought blacks to these shores against their will, Sowell suggested that if payments were in order for the *consequences* of the forced migration it would make as much sense to demand them from American blacks themselves, for the opportunities they acquired as a result of having been brought here. These conflicting visions provide a good introduction to the paradox of race relations in America today.

It is twenty-five years since the civil rights revolution and more than a century since the Civil War, yet Americans are still being harangued about their racial guilt over slavery and segregation, as though neither event had ever taken place. Race, Americans are constantly reminded, is the gravest problem they face as a nation and the heaviest burden of their democratic history.

Charges of "racism" were a central theme in the last presidential election, provoked by the famous TV spots about Willie Horton and liberal myopia on the subject of crime. Suspicions of racism are now key components of all hearings on Supreme Court appointments, with

---

This article first appeared in New Dimensions, *December 1990.*

liberal senators interrogating nominees about their views on poll taxes, voter literacy tests and the 14th Amendment, as though these issues had not been decided decades before. Editorial writers in the prestige press constantly warn Americans that they must support government programs to redress the outstanding and seemingly endless grievances of the black community lest dire, yet "understandable," consequences ensue — as though opposition to welfare programs that have failed in the past were an act of racial prejudice worthy of punishment.

No one can doubt the truth of the proposition that race is a burden on the American conscience. No one would deny that the legal and institutional discrimination that was the legacy of American slavery required a national rethinking and a dramatic redress. But it has been a quarter of a century since the agonizing reappraisal and restitution took place. Why is America's conscience about race still the subject of such passionate attacks? Why are Americans — surely the most diverse, tolerant and generous of people — constantly being accused by their media and leaders of boundless racist sentiments and acts of oppression?

After all, most Americans over thirty have participated in or supported a political and cultural revolution without parallel in human history. In a single generation, discriminatory practices and segregationist laws in America have been declared unconstitutional and universally abolished. Martin Luther King, the black leader of this struggle to create civil equality for all Americans, is now a national hero — along with Washington and Lincoln, the only American to be specially honored with a national holiday. His dream of a future in which every individual would be "judged by the content of his character and not the color of his skin" has been integrated into the American dream in a way that only Lincoln's famous Gettysburg image — "a government of, by and for the people" — had been previously.

As dramatic as America's homage to Dr. King has been, its commitment to provide black Americans with full citizenship rights has been no less striking. Black Americans have become the mayors, police chiefs, and public officials of Birmingham, Selma and Atlanta, the very citadels of what was once the segregationist South. The mayor of Atlanta is himself a former civil rights activist, a lieutenant of Dr. King and a one-time U.S. ambassador to the United Nations.

Nor is it only in the South that such victories have been won. There are 5,000 elected black officials in the nation today, twenty *times* the number of twenty-five years ago. Black Americans have been elected mayors of the great metropolitan centers of New York, Chicago, Detroit, Newark, Philadelphia, Seattle, Cleveland, Washington and Los Angeles. If a black American has not yet been elected President, neither has a Jewish or Italian or Polish American, groups which have also been here for hundreds of years. A black American, Jesse Jackson, has been runner-up for the Democratic Party's presidential nomination; no Jewish or Italian or Polish American can even make that claim. It hardly seems presumptuous to conclude that in the last twenty years, black Americans have finally become an integral part of the nation's political life.

And not only its political life. Americans have entrusted their national security to a black American, Colin Powell, first as the president's national security adviser and now as the head of the nation's armed forces. In 1984, when America hosted the Olympics in Los Angeles, it chose a black athlete, Rafer Johnson, to light the ceremonial torch that opened the games. America's highest literary honor, the Pulitzer Prize, recently went to a black woman, Toni Morrison. For nearly a decade, a black family has been the most watched model family on American television and its black creator, Bill Cosby, television's highest paid star. America's top grossing film star, Eddie Murphy, is black; its top earning musician, Michael Jackson; its top TV talk show host, Oprah Winfrey; its highest paid athlete, Michael Jordan; its most celebrated new artistic talent, Spike Lee; and its most famous preacher-politician, Jesse Jackson. Year in, year out, the popular heroes of American culture — athletes, musicians, entertainers and film stars — the aristocracy of talent adored, emulated and worshipped as only royalty was in the past — are now significantly black Americans. All these signs would seem to confirm that the integration of black America into the national mainstream is a process well along the path to completion.

Yet Americans are constantly being told that the social, economic and political realities of American life serve to undermine or render insignificant the very meaning of these changes. A chorus of civil rights leaders even claims that America has made no real progress since the civil rights revolution, that black Americans lost ground in the "Reagan decade," that racism is as pervasive and the goal of equality as remote as ever. Here is Jesse Jackson sounding off at the beginning of the year of his current campaign to be recognized as a world statesman and presidential heir apparent:

> Ronald Reagan took the shame and guilt out of racism....The brutal ideology that was set back by the Civil War, Reconstruction and the civil rights movement has returned with tremendous force during the past decade. Racism is now so powerful again in our domestic and foreign policy that it threatens the soul of our nation and our status as leader of the Free World.

This is a preposterous caricature of American government and America's reality. Yet it is true that the racial consciousness of the American public has become higher in the last few years than at any time since the Sixties. The signs are numerous. The founder of the National Association for the Advancement of White People, David Duke, is a leading Republican politician in Louisiana. In major cities like Chicago and New York, black Americans have recently voted in blocs of over 90% for black candidates, regardless of politics. Despite the fact that Jesse Jackson is a Democratic leader and a self-styled moral spokesman against racial prejudice, during last year's Chicago mayoral election he urged black voters to bolt the Democratic Party and vote for an independent candidate because Chicagoans "needed" a mayor who was black.

In recent years, racial crimes like the Howard Beach incident, the killing of Yussuf Hawkins and the "wilding" in Central Park have occupied the front pages of the nation's press almost without reprieve. Scores of racial incidents have troubled the liberal campuses of UCLA, the University of Michigan, the University of Massachusetts, Columbia, Dartmouth and other Ivy League schools where they were once nonexistent. At City University in New York a white professor, Michael Levin, writes scholarly articles about the genetic inferiority of blacks, while a black professor, Leonard Jeffries, teaches undergraduates about the moral superiority of the "sun people" who have a high melanin content in their skin and are thus better than the "ice people" who are white. Everywhere one turns — on college campuses, on radio talk shows, in the press, in the streets — one finds demagogues spreading conspiracy theories of the most sinister import, and gaining a significant audience among the public at large.

How can there be two such different Americas — the one increasingly integrated and publicly committed to the equal rights of all its citizens, the other marching towards separate societies and the brink of racial confrontation?

At the root of this paradox is a new politically inspired racism. While the old racism may have served economic and social interests, its root sources were instinctive and visceral. White crackers, Ku Klux Klanners and assorted neo-Nazis of the old school believed in the genetic inferiority of other groups and yearned to be rid of them or — failing that — to repress them. This is the racism that America fought wars against abroad and defeated at home.

But there is a new racism abroad in America today. It is politically inspired and seeks the enactment of laws that are racially specific and tailored to the requirements of selected groups; it attributes the economic, social and moral problems of designated minorities to their alleged "oppression" by a rigged System; and it seeks to solve their problems by the exaction of public ransoms in the form of government benefits and special privilege for ethnic grievance. This new racism has sprung up and spread like a poisonous weed to choke the civility that the civil rights movement established. It has given the old racism a new lease on life.

The function of a civil order is to humanize the behavior of its citizens and elevate their souls, to restrain their impulses to savagery and evil. That is the significance of the laws that were instituted by the civil rights revolution under the leadership of Martin Luther King. By making America's standards color blind and universal, they completed the Constitutional covenant and reaffirmed its principles and ideals: they called America to its better self.

But it was never in their capacity to remake Americans, to extirpate the reflexes of fear and resentment of the Other, that achieve their repulsive apotheosis in racism, and that are inscribed in the character of all human beings like a malignant genetic code. Just as the impulse to sin does not disappear with religion, so barbarism does not vanish with civilization. It can only be held at bay and driven underground. The old racism did not die with the advent of civil rights; it was civilly suppressed. That is the significance of the civil rights revolution, and why defending its principles is more urgent than ever.

For these principles are now under siege by the new political racism, whose malignancy rises from the Marxist cauldrons of the radical Left. Its immediate target is white "establishment" America, but its ultimate victims are poor and black.

America became familiar with the voice of this racism in a series of controversial criminal investigations in which racial issues were pushed to the fore. In the most memorable of these — the Howard Beach and Tawana Brawley incidents — the pattern was identical: A racial crime was committed — or, in the case of Tawana Brawley who claimed to have been raped and mutilated by a gang of whites — allegedly committed. But in each case the law was blocked in its efforts to investigate the circumstances of the crimes. And in each case, the forces that blocked their efforts were the radical attorneys for the victims themselves. They refused to allow their clients to cooperate with the law in the prosecution of the crimes, claiming justice would not be done, indeed *could not* be done, because the System was in its very nature racist and unjust. Thus, the crimes became the occasions not for indictments of the deranged individuals who might have actually committed them, but of America itself. (Did these accusations seem like the paranoid responses of the political fringe? Tawana Brawley and her lawyers, later exposed by investigators as liars and frauds, were supported by a broad-based public in the black community including celebrities like Bill Cosby, who donated tens of thousands of dollars to their cause.)

The indictment of America as a racist oppressor has been heard before. It is the prosecutorial brief of the radical Left. In the Sixties it was the legal strategy of every radical on trial from Panther leader and murderer Huey Newton to the guerilla conspirators of the "Chicago 7." Newton's Marxist lawyer, Charles Garry, who devised the defense strategy of "putting the System on trial" titled his autobiography *Street-fighter in the Courtroom*. When Bobby Seale and a group of Black Panthers in New Haven, Connecticut were indicted for the torture-murder of Alex Rackley, student radicals at Yale shut down the university and demanded that their trial be stopped. So fevered was the political atmosphere of the time, that these student nihilists were actually joined in their demands by Yale President Kingman Brewster, who later explained to the media that "a black person cannot get a fair trial in America today." (This turned out to be a true statement if the black person, like Alex Rackley, had the misfortune of being murdered by the Left. For though they had admitted participating in the torture, the Panther leaders were not convicted.)

The radical lawyers for Tawana Brawley and the Howard Beach defendants — Vernon Mason and Alton Maddox — learned their courtroom strategies during the Sixties in the liberation schools of the radical Left. Both Mason and Maddox were trained by William Kuntsler, undisputed dean of "revolutionary" lawyers — comrade-in-arms and advocate for Abbie Hoffman, Tom Hayden and the Chicago 7 (whom he collectively compared to Jesus Christ), attorney and political sympathizer for the cop-killing terrorists of the Black Liberation Army, and today counsellor for the "wilding" rapists of Central Park.

It is because the new racism is a bastard child of the political Left that it has gone largely unnoted by social commentators and generally unreported in the nation's press. There are historical grounds for this myopia. Racist movements have long been associated in the public mind with the political Right, while the Left has been seen as a champion of oppressed minorities and civil rights. But even these facile associations reflect a distorted perspective. Thus "populism," the most successful Leftist movement in America's past, eventually degenerated into segregationist politics, while Nazism, the most significant racist movement of the 20th Century (though generally labelled a movement of the Right), was radically anti-capitalist and socialist from the start.

A more solid ground for the impression that the Right is properly associated with racial politics while the Left pursues goals of social integration is the history of the civil rights revolution itself. Although the old Marxist Left had once advocated black separatism and a "black nation" (to be made up of several states in the American South), it changed its attitude for opportunistic reasons in the Forties and Fifties and provided crucial support for the integrationist push. It is also true that most conservatives, defending the principles of state's rights and private contract, initially opposed the civil rights revolution and thus lent their political weight to the old racism in its last ditch stand.

But the last twenty-five years have brought dramatic changes in the political landscape affecting both Right and Left, at home and abroad. The civil rights revolution is now a long accomplished fact, ratified in America's social consciousness and solidly inscribed in American law. American conservatives not only have come to accept the wisdom of the revolution they once resisted, but have become its staunchest political defenders. In battle after battle over affirmative action proposals and other post-civil rights efforts by liberals to introduce racial categories and quotas into the laws of the land, it is conservative legislators who have insisted that the law be "color blind" and it is conservative presidents and Supreme Court justices who have attempted through their veto power to hold the line.

But more important even than these changes in the complexion of the political Right have been the changes that have taken place on the political Left. No sooner was the civil rights revolution written into law than the radical Left was agitating to overthrow it. "Integration" was derided as "Uncle Tomism" and "co-optation"; "Black Power" became the slogan of the radical agenda. Martin Luther King was now a legend of the discarded past; Malcom X was the prophet of the radical future.

This progression was inevitable. Radicals are the permanently unsatisfied among us, the resentful nihilists of the utopian cause. Restless with the imperfections of humanity as they find it, radicals clamor for a future in which human beings will be different and the world will be transformed. In the radical future, racism and other evils will be miraculously purged from the species forever, and of course the radicals themselves will inherit the earth. But, first, society must be polarized and all existing structures destroyed. This is the secular messianism that has blighted the century, the malevolent "idealism" that subverts its own ends and leads instead to the Nazi gas chambers and the Communist gulag.

For old style liberals and contemporary conservatives, politics is fundamentally the art of compromise. For radicals it is war by other means. The civil war of radical politics begins by dividing society into opposing camps: victims and victimizers, oppressors and oppressed. This war can end only with the annihilation of the social enemy, which ushers in the millennium of social peace.

In launching a civil war in which victory must be total, radicalism reveals itself as a species of racism. Communism and fascism are kissing cousins: the stigmatization of entire social groups, whether capitalists or Jews, is combined with the will to suppress them permanently in the name of a better world.

Marxism long appeared to be free from racist taint because the messianic force on which it pinned its hopes was not an ethnic or racial group, but an economic *class*. But in the Sixties, radicals lost all hope that the working class would ever become a revolutionary force. Instead, they transferred their destructive faith to substitute candidates: women, gays and blacks. It was in this crucible that radical feminism, and the gay and black liberation movements of the New Left were forged. In the American South, the emergence of this Left, under the leadership of Stokeley Carmichael and the Black Power activists, derailed the integration process and the civil rights agenda. Guided by radicals like Carmichael, the Movement that had once fought for an integrated America became anti-white and anti-Semitic and anti-American as well.

Martin Luther King had believed in American democracy, and had fought for a single American standard: one justice indivisible, for all. He had embraced the historic alliance between blacks and Jews, America's other outcast minority, and championed the cause of American pluralism. Carmichael hated America and American democracy, hated Jews and hated whites and expelled them from the civil rights coalition, preaching black separatism and black power. The goal of integration — the classic route to success in America — was condemned by the new black radicals as a path to moral corruption and political co-optation; the path of equal opportunity was dismissed as a mirage; the strategies of non-violence and compromise were rejected in favor of a politics of confrontation and threat; the political model of the civil rights struggle ceased to be one of moral persuasion and became one of civil war.

At the end of the Sixties when violent revolution failed to materialize, Carmichael deserted his constituents and went into exile as a prince across the water in Marxist Guinea. In his adopted homeland, the atrocities committed by the government against its impoverished African population were acceptable to him because the dictator was a friend, a socialist and black. But in the last decade, as the seeds he had sown in the Sixties began to sprout their poisonous blooms, Carmichael returned to spread his message of anti-Americanism, anti-Semitism and black racism on campuses across the United States, where he was welcomed by the New Left professoriate and its student disciples.

For more than a decade, activists like Carmichael have been stars of the campus circuit, indoctrinating new generations in the divisive and racially polarizing ideologies of the radical Left, and in denigrating American values and institutions. They have been supported by a chorus of white New Left academics and accommodating administrators who find their rantings congenial. Indeed the universities themselves have been transformed by the New Left into staging areas for the radical future.

When the guerrillas of the Sixties marched off the streets and into the universities at the end of the decade, they did not demand "proletarian studies" programs to advance their Marxist class agendas. Instead they demanded Black Studies, Women's Studies, Native American Studies, and Gay and Lesbian Studies. These new "disciplines" for which there were no intellectual standards or academic traditions provided an ideal proving ground for their revised ideologies of political warfare — feminism, black nationalism and gay liberation. Rather than becoming institutions of scholarly research, the new "Studies Centers" became intellectual fortresses from which to launch new assaults on America's values and American culture.

In the 1960s Amiri Baraka, a.k.a. Leroi Jones, was a radical loud-mouth, writing diatribes like this: "We want poems like fists beating niggers out of Jocks of dagger poems in the slimy bellies of the owner-jews. Look at the Liberal Spokesman for the jews clutch his throat and puke himself into eternity/Another bad poem cracking steel knuckles in a jewlady's mouth." Today, thanks to the new cultural diversity in the American Academy, Amiri Baraka is chairman of the Afro-American Studies Department at the prestigious Stonybrook campus of the State University of New York. At Stonybrook Baraka has found a tenured platform from which to denounce America and to praise its global enemies. Nor is he untypical. Cornel West is a professor of "Afro-American Studies" at Princeton University, earning perhaps $70,000 a year. Writing in the Leftist magazine *Tikkun*, recently, Professor West described himself as "an Afro-American freedom fighter." While this is revealing of the rich fantasy life of the professorial Left, it also reflects its sinister agenda: to convince black students that America is a racist oppressor and that the real solution is war.

It is this campus Left that has promulgated the idea that there is no common cultural heritage that belongs to all Americans; that the culture out of which this democracy was conceived is really the culture of a master race; that the American consensus is oppressive in its very nature, in the same way that American justice is oppressive, that American institutions are inherently racist and need to be replaced.

The appeal to philosophical principle and abstract theory is the high road taken by New Left academics in their assault on the covenants that, until now, have made America's democracy the wonder and envy of the world. But there is a low road, as well, on which popular demagogues have followed after them, inspired by their indictments and encouraged by their attacks. From Susan Sontag's infamous thesis of the 1960s that "The white race is the cancer of history," to Black Muslim Elijah Muhammad's revelation that whites are devils invented by a mad scientist named Yakub, is no great leap at all.

The largest and most powerful racist organization in the United States today is the Nation of Islam, a pseudo-religious political cult, founded by Louis Farrakhan and born out of the same malevolent crucible as the Sixties Left. Today, Farrakhan is a favorite campus speaker of Black Student Unions across the country, commanding $10,000 fees for spreading his gospel of racist pride and hate. For Farrakhan, as for the liberation theologians of the radical Left, the political is religious. Thus, he and his followers regard white America and its Jews as great Satans conspiring to commit genocide against the black population through the epidemics of drugs and AIDS. In a recent speech broadcast as a public service by Leftist station KPFK, Farrakhan lieutenant Steve Coakely even identified the local measles epidemic in Los Angeles as part of this genocidal plot.

In his diatribe, Coakely also touched a radical theme that has been showcased for national audiences in Spike Lee's *Do The Right Thing*. Coakely claimed that white America was killing blacks with impunity.

The problem with black people, he complained, was that "we don't deliver retribution," which could also be a subtext of Lee's film. ("Tawana Brawley Told The Truth" was a slogan scrawled across one of its frames.)

At a recent public gathering in the heart of the nation's capital, with former civil rights hero and disgraced Mayor Marion Barry on the podium as an object lesson, "Minister Farrakhan" worked his black audience preparing them for the coming race war. Invoking the "persecution" of American blacks over the centuries, he pointed to Barry as the most recent example and ranted: "All white America could be asked to die to equal the score."

Racist hatemongers like Farrakhan and Coakely, and their genocidal messages, far from being stigmatized and isolated on the political fringe, have — through the intervention of the Left, the tolerance of the civil rights establishment and the acquiescence of the liberal center — become part of the culture itself. The claim that there is a governmental/white conspiracy against blacks in America has been a weapon in the rhetorical arsenal of the Left for two decades. It is as readily found in the editorials of the Leftist *Nation* (which have routinely claimed that the war on drugs is a war on black America), as in the public utterances of literary icons like Toni Morrison, who told *Time* magazine that the only thing binding America together, as a nation, was its racism towards American blacks.

Embracing the general idea of genocidal conspiracy supported by radical academic theorists obviously makes it easier to accept the specific paranoias spread by demagogues like Farrakhan about drugs and AIDS. But the grotesque libels have themselves been propounded by tenured radicals as though they were facts, and disseminated in "news" stories by Left-wing journalists like Earl Caldwell of New York's *Daily News*. Even as responsible a black columnist as William Raspberry of the Washington *Post* has defended Farrakhan on the spurious grounds that he has some true things to say (as though Hitler did not). Nor has the outcry against these genocidal libels been all that deafening. Jesse Jackson, while still the leading Democratic politician in Chicago, chose to be silent during the public storm that broke after it was revealed that Coakely — then a $70,000 a year aide to the Democratic mayor — had accused Jewish doctors of injecting blacks with AIDS. Widely regarded as a moral leader, Jackson can condemn the President of the United States as a racist, while refusing to make similar judgements of Coakley, the Nation of Islam or Farrakhan, his continuing friend and political ally.

Silences like Jackson's are made easy and thus virtually inevitable by the liberal center's collusive tolerance of the new racism. This tolerance ranges from allowing political demagogues to posture as moral spokesmen while maintaining their ties to bigots like Farrakhan, to portraying those bigots as social critics. Thus a *New York Times* story described Washington Mayor Marion Barry's alliance with Farrakhan in these self-parodying terms: "[Barry] has shown up at rallies with the Rev. Louis Farrakhan, the Nation of Islam leader who has gained nationwide attention for his criticism of white society, particularly Jews."

Mayor Barry's alliance with Farrakhan was but the latest episode in the series of Reichstag fire incidents that began with the fraudulent claims of Tawana Brawley and escalated afterwards, in which the normal processes of the judicial system are converted by Left-wing racists and black "nationalists" into their standard morality play about oppressive "Amerikkka" ruled by white devils and in need of liberation. The success of this morality play is such that the truly genocidal libel that whites and Jews are plotting the destruction of black Americans is now given wide credence in black communities across the country, in the way similar conspiracy libels against the CIA and other government agencies have become staples of belief in the communities of the Left.

A recent Los Angeles *Times* report on the spread of conspiracy theories in the black community quoted Wilbert Tatum, editor and publisher of New York's oldest and largest black paper, the *Amsterdam News*, as believing that the federal government was involved in a secret plot with Latin American drug kingpins and Mafia bosses to flood inner-city neighborhoods with narcotics as a form of genocide against blacks. When asked for evidence, Tatum could only cite the "authentic language" of a scene in the film "The Godfather," in which a Mafia don decides to push drugs to blacks. William Cavil, associate director of the Institute for the Advanced Study of Black Family Life and Culture in Oakland, California was quoted in the same report as saying "I don't understand, if there's not some conspiracy going on, how every group has managed to flourish and get ahead in the country except African-Americans," and Barbara Sizemore, a black studies professor at the University of Pittsburgh, as concluding "I no longer think it's a conspiracy....I call it outright war."

The conquest of the political culture of the black community by the radical Left has allowed hatemongers like Farrakhan to gain an acceptance and support among blacks that is truly alarming. It far exceeds the acceptance of any comparable figure including the most popular social prophet among today's black youth, the late Malcolm X. Although it is generally forgotten now, during his lifetime Malcolm X was condemned and isolated by Martin Luther King and the broad leadership of the black civil rights movement precisely because of his rhetorical violence and racist agendas. (And with positive effect: in the last year of his life, Malcolm abandoned the racist creed of his Black Muslim past.)

The liberal center is now so permeated by the culture of the Left that institutions like the *Times* and the *Washington Post* (which recently presented Farrakhan's views in a lengthy, respectful format suited to a world important statesman) are unable to recognize the enemies of liberal society for what they are. As a result, they legitimize by default "community leaders" whose civic agenda is to provoke a race war. Of course, this liberal myopia applies only to hatemongers in one direction. Grand Dragons of the Ku Klux Klan and neo-Nazis, with parallel ideas, can expect no such respectful receptions.

The double standard has led to ugly consequences: the legitimization of white racist rhetoric in the advocacy of reverse affirmative action among ordinary Americans who don't necessarily read the *Times*; the reemergence of white racism as a political program in the candidacy of former klansman David Duke. In a political atmosphere in which preferential treatment and race-based laws are advocated by the liberal establishment, a National Association for the Advancement of White People can begin to look like an equal opportunity party.

In fact, this revitalization of the old racism is integral to the agenda of the Left, because it is the key to its favored strategy, which is to eliminate the moderate center. Thus, in the early Seventies, Angela Davis formed a Communist Party front called the Alliance Against Racism whose main target was the Ku Klux Klan. At the time, the Klan was a thoroughly discredited, closely monitored and generally moribund institution. Shortly afterwards, a mini-sect calling itself the Communist Workers Party announced a "Death to the Klan" rally in Greensboro North Carolina, provoking a gun battle in which five of their own members were killed. At the time, the Klan was hardly important. But it was vital to the political strategy of Leftists like Angela Davis and the Communist Workers Party that the Klan *be* important. For it is only when the political situation becomes polarized that the radical agenda can begin to seem reasonable to ordinary people.

Historically, in fact, the way to every Leftist political victory has been paved by the elimination of the political middle. Only when the Left can present itself as the lone alternative to a fascist Right has victory been within its grasp. In the last two decades the Left has greatly eroded the liberal center on the issue of race. The Democratic Party has been almost completely captured by the agenda of affirmative action and racial preference. In California, the Democratic candidate for governor in 1990 began her campaign by declaring that she would staff her administration according to racial quotas. For nearly three decades, the Left has relentlessly assaulted the American ethos — the idea of universal standards, of equal opportunity and of competitive reward. The task that faces Americans is to defend those principles by reaffirming their faith in American justice, by condemning and isolating racist hatemongers, and by rejecting the radical Left, both black and white, which uses politics as a means of civil war. ☐

IV

The Nineties: Leftover Leftism

Chapter One

America After Reagan

(Peter Collier)

If the Reagan era had offered us nothing more than a breathing space, we should be grateful. Its accomplishments were, of course, far greater than that. Even before the President's term comes to a formal close, it is hard not to be suffused with a sense of loss and nostalgia. Yet as I think about the subject of what comes next, I find myself feeling — to use an analogy from my California youth — like a surfer who has watched with anxious anticipation as a huge wave comes rolling up, only to see it pass leaving an unchanged sea. What I am getting at is that there are certain things — things that should concern us greatly — that the Reagan revolution scarcely affected at all. I'm talking primarily about the Leftism which I believe may be the wave in our future, a wave that will not leave our seas unchanged.

Some of you are possibly wondering what I have in mind when I refer to "Leftism." It is not that easy to "define the terms," as we used to say in college, when we are talking about a phenomenon in which people refuse to admit who they are and what they are for. I'm reminded of an article written a few years ago by a professed Leftist named Christopher Hitchens who functions, with Alexander Cockburn, another English expatriate, as the Burgess and Maclean of the *Nation* magazine. This article happened to be about terrorism. Hitchens' basic position seemed to be that the retaliations of Israel were as much terrorist acts as the attacks of the PLO that occasioned them, and that the defensive maneuvers of the West were terrorist in the same sense as the aggressions of the Soviet bloc. The conclusion he wanted us to draw was that since terrorism is everywhere equally, it is therefore nowhere in particular and thus it makes no sense to single out the Palestinians

---

Speech to a conference of the Committee On The Free World, November 18-22, 1989.

or Syrians or Libyans. If you can't define it, went the chop logic, it must not exist. To which one might answer, as my friend and writing partner David Horowitz did, "I can't define the color red either, but I know it when I see it."

I know Leftism when I see it and so should you. It is not liberalism, that confused term and abused faith. Liberals, at least those worthy of the term, became obsolete with the 1968 riots at the Democratic convention in Chicago. Those who had been the vital center of American politics in the postwar world became exiles in their own party. Their place was taken by figures like Tom Hayden and Jesse Jackson, who had little in common with traditional liberalism, which in fact they had considered the enemy. These people might call themselves liberal when it suits them; they might use the legacy of Robert Kennedy and Martin Luther King when it is convenient. But really they have nothing in common with liberalism and everything in common with the "progressivism" of people in the streets demonstrating in behalf of the Sandinistas and the FMLN, and with the people in the academy and in the media who agree that America is inexorably racist and elitist at home and imperialist and homicidal in its foreign policy. These assumptions and the policies based on them are what contemporary Leftism is all about. It is a movement obsessed with American guilt and excited by thoughts of American impotence. It is a sensibility in solidarity with Third World totalitarianism which it insists is merely nationalism under assault. It is a mentality which uses the term "McCarthyism" as a bludgeon to beat into silence those who would try to find its hidden agendas or strip its deceitfully layered apparatus.

Most of us experience Leftism without knowing it. It is the political white sound, the ideological elevator music playing in the background of our lives. Leftist cliches vulgarize our intellectual environment. Thus in a post-mortem on the recently concluded Olympic Games, one commentator solemnly complained that the Third World, which represents 80% of the world's population, had won only 12% of the medals at Seoul. One was left to contemplate the remedy — affirmative action that would insure a place on the victory stand for backstrokers from Uganda, Indonesian discus throwers, and Syrian equestrian riders.

Leftism is the computer virus of popular culture. We neo-conservatives may be thankful for Chuck Norris and Tom Selleck, Conan and Rambo; but they are individuals in Hollywood while Leftism is a movement. Jane Fonda and her husband have been so successful in building cadre in the finishing school they run for the so-called Brat Pack, that whenever there is an election, they are able to unleash busloads of these people — heavy thinkers like Rob Lowe and Morgan Fairchild and Moon Zappa — on the people of my state in the service of progressive causes. These people and their elders are the ones who served up Daniel Oretega like an exotic *hors d'oeuvre* at their cocktail parties a few years ago and now that the struggle has shifted to El Salvador serve up Reuben Zamorra. These are the people who see it as an act of commitment to produce a film like *Running On Empty*, which backhandedly celebrates the bombers of the Sixties by portraying them as the Ozzie and Harriet of the underground.

It would be easy to dismiss the Leftism of these film personalities as the political equivalent of a fashion statement. But the industry itself — America's Dream Factory — has been infected with the cliches they mouth. There is an informal censorship which means that a film like *The Hanoi Hilton*, which dissents from prevailing orthodoxy, doesn't get exhibited. There is a sense of mission so strong that the studios often don't even act in their own interest, continuing to turn out box office failures like *Walker* and Costa-Gavras' *Betrayed* because they have "good politics." And if you think that these same impulses do not exist at a higher brow level you apparently did not catch Bill Moyers' recent PBS interview with Noam Chomsky in which the man who is arguably the fountainhead of radical anti-Americanism in our time was treated as a sort of home-grown Aristotle.

We live in a popular culture which suspended the fairness doctrine a long time ago. It is getting less even-handed year by year. Thus we have the network anchormen moaning sanctimoniously about Bush's "negative campaigning" in the recent election, while they said scarcely a word about the most negative campaign of them all, the one by the mis-named People for the American Way to blacken the character of Robert Bork. It is easy for us to dismiss movies and television as so much tinsel and glitter. But it is where the battle for the future is being waged — a battle not just for minds and hearts but for what we define as decent and right. It is a battleground on which we have been doing poorly enough and will do even worse after Reagan.

Leftism advances unimpeded in other areas of our national life as well. Think of the American university, where there are now, as Walter Laqueur has noted, more Marxists than there are in the Soviet Union. The academic environment is greatly influenced, if not controlled outright, by one-time New Leftists and fellow travelers now at the midpoint of what the German Leftist Rudi Dutschke once advocated as a "long march through the institutions." Once they tried to burn the universities down. Now, without an ideological pause, they sit on the tenure committees which decide who will teach. They remake the curriculum in a process which would substitute Harriet Beecher Stowe for *Huckleberry Finn* and Ethnic Studies for Western Civilization. They create an ambiance in which American history and institutions are academic targets of opportunity; in which grievance has displaced scholarship, and in which the model for the ideal university administrator is a combination of Saul Alinsky, Mother Teresa, and Neville Chamberlain.

Twenty-five years ago I, along with others in the Free Speech Movement at Berkeley, lectured our professors about the need for Leftism. It is a measure of how things have changed that today the process is exactly reversed. The message comes from indirect and unlikely sources — the English Department, for instance, which decrees that a major must take a class in "colonial literature" lest he otherwise slip through without reading the second-rate works of the oppressed. In my last conversation with my son, who goes to Berkeley today, he said, "It is getting worse every day, Dad." I believe that this is so. The people who oppose the politicization of the university — the good people of the center who care about standards and truth — consider themselves a vanishing species and walk the groves of academe in wistful resignation.

When I grew up the adversary culture was in an adversary position. Now it is the dominant culture. It no longer tells subversive truths — if indeed it ever did. Now it inculcates anti-American orthodoxies and enforces theories of our national guilt and corruption. Now it suppresses views different from its own far more ruthlessly than the hated "confor-

mism" of my youth ever did, and it batters the common sense prag-
matism that has always been this country's most attractive feature and
may be its last best hope. In America after Reagan *we* are the adversary
culture, and we had better start acting like it.

Leftism, of course, is not just in our popular and intellectual culture
but in our political culture as well. Arthur Schlesinger tells us that
political styles are cyclical and just as the "conformism" of Ike led to
JFK's New Frontier, so the clamped down conservatism of Reagan has
created the Left resurgence whose growing evidence we now see all
around us.

In fact, this resurgence should be seen as intentional rather than
inertial. Like the slowly metamorphosing monster of horror films, the
Left was recreating itself during the apparent dormancy following the
end of the Sixties. If there is a pendulum, it works less by the laws of
motion than by the laws of Leftism itself, which has alternated between
militant extremism and popular fronting moderation since its inception.
The current revival will not bring violent revolutionaries into the streets
as in the Sixties. No, the current offensive of "progressivism" — that
odious euphemism — has as its target that fraction of the Democratic
Party not already under its control, the church, the university, and other
institutions traditionally associated with liberalism and individual
freedom and anti-Communism.

Leftism has a tremendous advantage. In our world view democracy's
losses are traumatic, if not permanent. For the Left, today is the first day
of the rest of their lives. Losses are merely temporary setbacks, stations
of the cross on the march toward the inevitable triumph of utopia. No
matter the body count in Southeast Asia as a result of the policies of the
Left, both in this country and over there, they move on to Central
America ready to force the same disasters on the unwitting peasants of
that region that have failed so miserably elsewhere. *Hasta la victoria
siempre.* "Two, three, many Vietnams. Vietnam has won, Nicaragua will
win. Nicaragua has won, El Salvador will win. Two, three, many
Nicaraguas..."

Is there any doubt what the Left's agenda is in the era to come? El
Salvador is at the top of the list. We can see the transition from the

struggle in Nicaragua to the one in El Salvador being made as if in time lapse before our very eyes. They tried to turn El Salvador over to the FMLN before and were beaten back. They contented themselves with consolidating their gains in Nicaragua and biding their time. That time is now. We can expect the same campaign. Committees of anguished intellectuals using the death squads as an excuse to de-couple the U.S. from El Salvador at the same time that organizations like CISPES — a front set up by the Salvadoran guerrillas themselves which the FBI is prohibited from keeping under surveillance — takes to the streets and campuses with its message of disinformation. This collaboration between the intellectuals and the activists — an ideological Mutt and Jeff act — will be buttressed by the Leftism that has infiltrated Congress in the person of individuals such as Rep. Ronald Dellums, that good friend of Maurice Bishop and Fidel Castro, and Sen. Thomas Harkin, who went to Manauga and, at the request of the Sandinistas, tried to get Violetta Chamorro to open *La Prensa* under conditions of censorship.

And where, one might ask, will there be a countervailing force? At least during the Reagan years there was an Elliot Abrams to contradict those at home who acted as a fifth column in behalf of the *comandantes* and to debate the Sandinistas given easy access to American television. Now that the Reagan era is over, who will speak these ideas? Who will be the countervailing force in the Bush administration during the certain attempts to destabilize El Salvador? One would feel better about an answer evolving for this question if the president-elect had not ignored Central America during his campaign, not even mentioning the fact, for instance, that his opponent was on record as saying that he would live with Soviet client states in this hemisphere.

America after Reagan. A time when the successes of the past eight years will seem glorious in retrospect and the missed opportunities all the more tragic. We will see how much we have to be thankful to the president for. But one thing which we are well done with, in my opinion, is the incorrigible optimism of the last eight years that made things seem better than they were. A while back, my friend David Horowitz and I had lunch with a couple of White House speechwriters. The conversation naturally turned to presidential phrase-making. We said that we thought that one of the truly good images of the post-war era was JFK's "long twilight struggle." Surprisingly, these Reagan speechwriters said they hated it. Why? we asked. They said that it was too negative. "People need hope," one of them said. "They want to feel good." Not surprisingly, for them the great line of contemporary presidential speech making was, "It is morning in America."

It is only a short step in thought — even if it is a long one in rhetoric, from "Morning in America" to "Don't Worry, Be Happy." As we look at the period ahead — the period after Reagan — I think that we will have to learn to call things by their right names, whether we are talking about sleaze artists or crooks or communists. I think we will have to be more vigilant about Leftism and more concerned about what it is doing. And we will need to tell people what time it is by opening the shades and letting the twilight gleam in. ☐

Chapter Two

From Red To Green

(David Horowitz)

In the two hundred years since the French Revolution, conservatives have been waging a rearguard struggle in defense of freedom against the forces of the radical Left. For a hundred years this political combat has taken the form of an international civil war instigated by the Marxist heirs of Robespierre and Saint-Just against the democratic market societies of the West. We are now witnessing the triumphant end of the Marxist epoch that began with the Bolshevik coup in 1917 and that is being drowned by cries of freedom across the whole expanse of the Soviet empire seventy-two years later.

It was the events in France that introduced the word "revolution" into our political vocabulary as a term meaning the absolute break with an existing order and the establishment of a radically new one: a government of Virtue to replace the despotism of Tradition, a cult of Reason to replace the religions of Faith, the true order of Nature to replace the artificial system of Society. It was no coincidence, therefore, that the French Revolution also introduced the concept and practice of political terror. For behind the radical impulse is a consciousness alien to all that is human, rejecting the historically given needs and desires of ordinary people as "backward" and artificial — which is why the radical effort to maintain its order always requires radical force.

The radical differs from the reformer who seeks only to right particular wrongs; the radical seeks to annihilate the social order itself. His rebellion, in the words of Marx, is "not against any wrong in particular but against wrong as such." It is this idea that produces the radical's alienation from humanity, "an idea [in the words of Gerhart Niemeyer] that implies a declaration of war by some men on the historical existence of all men." The total critique of society (the total

This chapter originally appeared in National Review, *March 19, 1990.*

deconstruction of society, as we might put it today) leads inexorably to the revolutionary praxis — "total hostility, total suspicion, total terror: totalitarian power."

What can justify the nihilism of the revolutionary agenda? Only a vision of the coming apocalypse. Only a vision of the existing order as totally unjustified, unnatural, destructive. *Better Red then Dead.* To those of us who were radicals in the Sixties, this famous slogan had a different meaning than it had for liberals to whom it signified choosing the lesser of two evils. For radicals it meant that if we did not achieve world socialism we would all soon be dead. Our radical idea was that capitalism engendered conflict and war; unless capitalism was destroyed, this would sooner or later mean the end of civilization itself. On the eve of Lenin's conquest of power, the German revolutionary Rosa Luxemburg summarized this vision of a radical apocalypse in the slogan "socialism or barbarism" — if mankind did not choose the socialist future, civilization would be destroyed by capitalist barbarism and its imperialist wars.

The apocalyptic claim is the cornerstone of radical politics. For if the cause is absolute, everything is permitted, and the real work of revolution — radical nihilism, the destruction of what is — can be carried out with no look back. Thus, in the name of everlasting peace, Marxists wage permanent revolutionary war; in the name of a final human liberation, they enslave entire nations; in the name of ultimate justice, they commit unparalleled crimes.

For more than seventy years the prospect of "socialism or barbarism" served to justify the destruction of the existing societies behind the Iron Curtain, to legitimize the institution of the Soviet future. But those seventy years of the socialist future have made Rosa Luxemburg's claim grotesque. Today — from Estonia to Armenia, from Alexanderplatz to Tiananmen Square — the sea of humanity liberated by Marxists itself proclaims: Socialism *is* barbarism.

Even as its own inhumanity and inefficiency consume revolutionary socialism in the East, however, a specter can be seen rising from its ashes in the West. The colors are no longer red but green, the accents are those of Malthus rather than Marx, but the missionary project is remarkably intact. The planet is still threatened, the present still condemned, redemption through radical politics still presses: *Better Green Than Dead*. In environmentalism radicals have found a new paradigm for the paradigm lost.

Thus, the official program of France's new Green Party echoes Rosa Luxemburg's apocalyptic cry: "The future will be green or will not be at all." And the program of Germany's Greens exhibits the distinctive accents of the totalitarian voice: "The politics of radical ecology embraces every dimension of human experience...the old age is giving way to the new." Or, in the blunter expression of the founder of American "social ecology," Murray Bookchin: "We can't heal the environment without remaking society."

The old radical Adam is back: the apocalyptic ambition, the destructive resentment, the totalitarian project. "From all the knowledge we now have about environmental issues," writes Jonathon Porritt, a spokesman for Britain's Ecology Party and the Director of Friends of the Earth, "the inevitable conclusion is that our way of life cannot be sustained...we cannot go on living as we do now." The revolutionary agenda requires a revolutionary strategy. When Porritt hears politicians saying that they care for the environment and therefore want to achieve "sustainable growth," it leaves him "spitting with rage." We cannot continue, he says, "with [our] same material living standard and at the same time be warriors on behalf of the planet."

Thus radical ecology leads to the familiar threat. The virtuous state must control and restrict social wealth and redistribute it according to the radical creed. In the radical view, property — the foundation of free societies — is mere theft, whose spoils are to be divided up. As Porritt argues: "We in the West have the standard of living we do only because we are so good at stripping the Earth of its resources and oppressing the rest of the world's people in order to maintain that wealth." To achieve ecological balance means "progressively narrowing the gap to reduce the differences between the Earth's wealthiest and poorest inhabitants" until there are "more or less equal shares for all people."

Karl Marx described this prescription aptly 150 years ago when he wrote: "Primitive communism is only the culmination of...envy and leveling down on the basis of a preconceived minimum. How little this abolition of private property represents a genuine appropriation is shown by [its] abstract negation of the whole world of culture and civilization, and [its] regression to the unnatural simplicity of the poor, rough man without wants, who has not only not surpassed private property but has not yet even attained to it."

Eco-socialism is barbarism.

Jonathon Porritt is a leader of the "moderate" wing of the radical environmental movement. David Brower, the founder of Porritt's organization, departed some years ago to create the more radical Earth Island Institute in Berkeley. Last June, Brower took his place alongside Comandante Daniel Ortega as co-sponsor of the Fourth Biennial meeting of the International Congress on the Hope and Fate of the Earth in Managua. One thousand delegates from more than seventy nations met at the Olaf Palme Center to denounce the United States and the other "imperialist" predators of the free world, and to launch a new movement of "solidarity environmentalism" by establishing alliances with radicals in Third World countries. According to a report in Brower's magazine: "The consensus at the Congress was that 'solidarity environmentalism' is the only kind that makes sense....Would George Bush and Margaret Thatcher be able to call themselves environmentalists if the effort to protect the ozone layer and stop global warming was linked to the Third World movement's demands for a new, more equitable international economic system, an end to the Third World debt, and curbs on the free action of multinational corporations?"

In Managua the political symbolism of the Green united front was all in place: Swedish social democracy, British Eco-socialism, Third World Marxism-Leninism, and American Auto-Nihilism. This development reflects the fact that the Green Movement has grown to its present dimensions out of the crisis of the Left — in particular the necessity of establishing a face-saving distance from the catastrophe of Marxist liberation in the socialist bloc. To avoid the taint of the socialist past, the Green parties of Europe and even primitive communists like Porritt, constantly emphasize that their movement is "neither Left nor Right," and distinguish the "politics of ecology" from the "politics of industrialism" (i.e., of economic growth) which characterize both capitalist and socialist societies. But from a historical perspective, it would be more accurate to say that the Green movement is a phenomenon of both the political Left *and* the political Right, uniting in itself the two traditions of radical totalitarian revolt against liberal order in the 20th Century — Communism and fascism — and aspiring to be the third wave of the gnostic assault against freedom in our lifetime.

The fascist roots of the Green movement are well known. National Socialists were naturists long before the post-Khrushchev Left discovered ecology, and the Nazis have been justly described as "the first radical environmentalists in charge of a state."[§] Indeed the enthronement of biological imperatives, of the virtues of blood and soil and the primitive communities of the Volk, the pagan rejection of the Judeo-Christian God and the radical anti-humanism featured in the philosophy of the Greens are even more obviously derivative of fascist than Marxist political traditions. But despite tensions that exist between the deep ecologists of the environmental Right-wing and the eco-socialists of its Left-wing, they are indissolubly joined in the common embrace of a single illusion: the gnostic idea that humanity has been alienated from its natural self and that its redemption can be achieved by political means; the idea that implies a declaration of war by a chosen few against the historical existence of all.

Thomas Lovejoy has expressed the radical anti-humanism of the Greens in a statement reminiscent of Susan Sontag's infamous indictment of the white race as the "cancer of history" during the Sixties: "The planet is about to break out into a fever and we are the disease." Appearing as a new ideological wrinkle at first, this turns out to be the same old anti-humanism of the radical tradition, the very malevolence that has brought it to its present grief. For there is no "true self" of mankind to be liberated, other than the historical self that we see manifest in its historical acts. The liberation of humanity in the sense of a restoration of its natural self is a radical myth. The radical reality is its assault on humanity as we know it. What motivates radicals is not compassion for the lost soul of mankind, but the hatred of human beings as they are. To the radical mind, whatever is is wrong.

[§]Cf.,M. Hauner, "A German Racial Revolution?" *Journal of Contemporary History,* Volume 19, 1984.

Ironically, however, it is this very antagonism to common humanity which, through the cunning of history, has proved to be the radicals' current undoing. In the name of injustice done to the proletariat, Marxists were able to carry out their work of destruction against bourgeois society. But once in power, Marxism — like fascism — exploited, oppressed and ruined the very masses it claimed to liberate. Having soared to power on dreams of transcendence, the radical enterprise succumbed to the gravitational pull of human nature, which even massive doses of terror and repression could not undo. The inability to remake humanity has now caused Marxism to founder in terminal crisis; the very victims in whose name its assault was carried out have now rejected it, so that Marxism can no longer speak in their name, nor invoke their suffering to justify its destructive agendas. This is the real crisis of the radical Left — and environmentalism is its solution.

In the environment, the Left has found a victim to champion that cannot reject it, a victim that will provide endless justification for its destructive agendas. This is the truly new element in the Green revolution: a constituency — nature — that cannot speak for itself. The conflict between vanguard and victim that has plagued generations of the Left has been thus eliminated. What remains is the hubris of the radical remnant, the self-chosen saviors for whom the human condition is not a reality we must come to terms with, but material which we must approach as gods and redeemers to subdue and transform.

What then is the conservative response to the environmental crisis and the radical threat? Conservatism is an anti-gnostic, anti-revolutionary attitude that accepts the fallen, unequal, alienated state of mankind and seeks to preserve the conditions of culture and freedom that human enterprise and moral imagination have created. The fact that conservatives recognize and accept the problematic nature of human existence does not mean that they embrace a passive attitude towards the problems of human societies. On the contrary their authentic concern about the fate and welfare of real human beings is attested by their two hundred-year struggle in defense of freedom. But now that the moment has come in which they are victors in this struggle and the Left lies defeated on the plain of battle, they must reemphasize the active, progressive side of the conservative project, accepting their responsibility as captains of the democratic ship of state. For, as Burke admonished, "a state without the means of some change is without the means of its conservation."

Conservatives should not surrender the defense of the environment to the Left, any more than we should surrender the defense of the Republic or of human rights to their historic enemies. Conservatives must not be blindly reactive, conceiving their role merely as a negative force, a check on radical hubris. Despite our commitment to liberty, indeed because of it, conservatives have maintained the peace and preserved the Republic, as the foundations of our freedom, by arming the state. Conservatives should not be afraid of the costs necessary to defend the environment, as a foundation of our communal health and human heritage. Not all growth is good. Metastasis is growth too. Nor is every event that calls itself a revolution bad. Two hundred years ago, conservatives took the lead in the American revolution to preserve their rights as Englishmen; today, they should take the lead in the reforms necessary to preserve the environment too. □

Chapter Three

The "Peace" Movement

(David Horowitz)

You see them every hour at the top of the local news with their signs of "No Blood for Oil," and their chants of "Hey, hey, ho, ho, George Bush has got to go." You watch their apologists, like aging New Leftist and TV pundit Todd Gitlin, squirm uncomfortably at their reckless passion in declaring America the enemy, while failing to condemn the global outlaw Saddam Hussein. You observe in mounting wonder as they descend on Washington to hear their balding Sixties heroes — Jesse Jackson, Daniel Ellsberg, Ron Kovic — call for capitulation on the battlefield and the impeachment of the president.

The troops in these demonstrations are dressed for battle in the old Movement issue (jeans and down jackets, lettered t-shirts, even tie-dyes); the familiar targets are steady in their sights: "big oil," the "Pentagon war machine" and "American imperialism." As always, they claim to be sheep in wolves clothing — despite the war paint, just pilgrims for peace. To disarm their critics, they volunteer their past "mistakes," like spitting on U.S. soldiers returning from Vietnam. Simultaneous with their present denunciations of U.S. "death squads" in Iraq, they maintain their heartfelt concern for the very soldiers who have volunteered to carry out the mission, and whose morale they continue to undermine.

Is the glaring contradiction between the belligerence and malice they project and their claims to good intentions the result of mere pig-headedness? An inability to communicate? Or is it the failure of their political camouflage to conceal the real motives that inform their passion? As a former partisan of similar movements, I never — in

This article appeared in National Review, *February 25, 1991.*

twenty-five years of political activism — marched in a demonstration that did not have primary agendas just beneath its pacifist surface that were militant, Marxist and anti-American. The "Coalition to Stop U.S. Intervention in the Middle East" (which staged the January 19 march on Washington) is but another cynical attempt by the now discredited Left to jump start the revolutionary engines that have recently stalled.

Do I exaggerate? Can the current mobilization be so readily dismissed as an occasion for America-bashing by the unrepentant Left? Consider the view of an unimpeachable source , a faithful keeper of the radical flame. Here is an excerpt from Alexander Cockburn's column in the December 31, 1990 *Nation*, commenting on the organizers of the Washington march:

> I wish people would stop writing to [suggest] that today leftists of principle should espouse the cause of Iraq and eschew criticism of Saddam Hussein. This is Marxism-Leninism-Bonkerism of a sort much savored by the Workers World Party, which seems to be the animating force behind the Coalition to Stop U.S. Intervention in the Middle East, decorated by Ramsey Clark. (*The Nation*, December 31, 1990)

Most people will not have heard of the Workers World Party, which according to Cockburn is the organization that has put together this new "anti-war" coalition. But I remember them from the Sixties as the only Trotskyist splinter to endorse the Soviet invasion of Hungary in 1956. Thus the spearhead of this season's "anti-war" demonstrations is a Marxist-Leninist party that defined itself by *supporting* the bloody invasion which took the lives of 30,000 Hungarians whose only crime was to want their national independence and freedom.

The anti-war Coalition favored by Cockburn was the National Campaign for Peace in the Middle East, which held its demonstration a week later on January 26th and was portrayed by the media as the 'liberal' peace contingent. But this turned out to be a distinction without a difference. Jesse Jackson, for example, addressed both demonstrations. The 'liberal' coalition was organized by the pathetic remnants of the American Communist Party and its fellow travelers and fronts, like the U.S. Peace Council. Its official coordinator was Leslie Cagan, a veteran

New Leftist, and — like the organizations that made up the coalition — pro-Castro, pro-Sandinista, pro-FMLN, pro-PLO and anti-American.

And it is the same story for the rank and file across the country. As a warm-up to the Washington demonstrations, activists held "teach-ins" from coast to coast, including one at Los Angeles' Fairfax High School, featuring Clark, Ellsberg, Kovic and Jackson. Attended by 1,500 people, the affair was described by the press as the largest "anti-war" demonstration until then. Its official spokesman, Achmed Nassef, told reporters that he had joined the Coalition through the Palestine Solidarity Committee. In other words, the official spokesman for the "peace" coalition was drawn from one of the only groups in the world supporting Saddam's rape of Kuwait.

Nassef also explained that the Coalition itself had grown out of groups that had been organized to oppose U.S. intervention in Central America — that is to say, of groups that proclaimed themselves "anti-war" when it came to the struggle of Nicaraguans against the Sandinista dictatorship, but *pro*-war when it came to the struggle of Communist guerrillas against an elected democracy in neighboring El Salvador. One of the headliners of the Fairfax High "teach-in" was Blase Bonpane, a defrocked priest who (like all the other speakers over fifty) had for three decades supported every Communist guerrilla war in the world. Bonpane even authored a book with the Orwellian title *Guerrillas for Peace*.

In addition to Achmed Nassef's Palestine Solidarity Committee, the "anti-war" Coalition sponsoring the teach-in included the Association of Palestinians for Return and the Committee for a Democratic Palestine — support groups for the PLO's terrorist war against the state of Israel. This led a reporter for *The Jewish Journal* to ask Bonpane whether the gathering was anti-Israel. "Why would someone say the gathering is anti-Israel?" Bonpane replied. "Because we're anti-war? We think that nothing would be worse for Israel than a war in the Middle East. We're horrified that some voices in Israel could be calling for this war." At a Santa Cruz teach-in two months earlier, Coalition members were even less careful in concealing their true animus, carrying signs that read "Zionism Kills" and "Palestinian Blood.")

These hypocrisies reminded me of the last time the Left tried to launch an anti-war crusade, which was when the Soviet Union invaded Afghanistan. It was then called a "Stop the War" movement, and its purpose was not to stop the Soviet invasion, but to oppose President Jimmy Carter's call for a resumption of the military draft, which he felt might be necessary to counter the Soviet aggression. This should be remembered every time the current peace Left hypocritically criticizes the present volunteer military as "undemocratic," since it was the opposition of the Left to a military draft during the Vietnam War and after that led to the creation of a volunteer Army in the first place. Of course what the Left really wanted — and what the Left still wants — is that the United States should have no army at all and should therefore be vulnerable to its Marxist enemies and their Marxist friends.

The Eighties Left, which opposed America's stand against Soviet aggression in Afghanistan, was no more "anti-war" than the present Left is. It was — like all the Lefts that have sprung up since the Sixties — anti-American. As the Soviet legions poured into Afghanistan in 1980, Leftist Congressman Ron Dellums (now the leader of the "anti-war" caucus in Congress) told the thousand cheering Berkeley students who had gathered for a "Stop the War" demonstration:

> From my vantage point, as your Representative, [I believe] we are at an incredibly dangerous moment. Washington D.C. is a very evil place...While [the White House] professes to see the arc of crises in Southwest Asia as the Balkan tinderbox of World War III, well Ron Dellums sees the only arc of crises being the one that runs between the basement of the west wing of the White House and the war room of the Pentagon.

America is the source of the world's crises and problems. This is the cardinal axiom of the Left. It was also, of course, the animating principle of the father of contemporary "anti-war" movements — the one that led to the victory in Indochina of Pol Pot and the Vietcong. In the words of a Santa Cruz student, active in the coalition:

> Obviously, this current anti-war movement takes inspiration from its Vietnam predecessor. Siphoned through twenty years of anti-Vietnam sentiments, my generation enters its movement more cynically than our counterparts of the Sixties...

More cynically indeed. For what did those "anti-Vietnam sentiments" accomplish, judged by the passage of those twenty years? A Communist-sponsored genocide in Indochina that extinguished nearly 2 million lives and obliterated a national culture. A decade and a half of Communist oppression in South Vietnam that killed more than a half million civilians, created nearly 1½ million refugees (unprecedented in Vietnam's 1,000-year history of foreign and domestic tyrannies) and made Communist Vietnam one of the poorest, most repressive and — let us not forget — militaristic states on the face of the earth.

This is the real agenda of today's anti-war radicals: to reprise the Vietnam experience of the Sixties in the Nineties. In fact, they can hardly wait to repeat it. "Right now our movement is not as big as Vietnam was,..." one student organizer breathlessly told a campus recruit, "[but] I think that as soon as a shooting war starts this will be even bigger than Vietnam." *Bigger than Vietnam.* This is what every radical for thirty years has dreamed of: an occasion that will trigger an explosion of the Left bigger than the Sixties itself.

And what is this Left? It is no longer a Left that pledges its allegiance to Soviet power and worships at the altar of the Soviet state — though it was that. It is no longer a Left that justifies Soviet expansion into Eastern Europe as a revolutionary beachhead of "peoples' democracies" — though it was that. It is no longer a Left that celebrates Chinese Communism as a new dawn in humanity's long march into the socialist future, or Cuba's gulag as a beacon of Latin America's coming liberation — though it was (and for some may still be) that.

It is a Left that has been disoriented by the repudiation of its socialist paradise by hundreds of millions of former inhabitants. But it is also a Left that has not for a single moment put down its weapons in the permanent war it has been waging, since 1917, against the capitalist societies of the democratic West, and in particular of the United States. Earlier this year, Daniel Singer — *The Nation's* authority on Eastern Europe — lectured Leftists as to how they should react to the rejection of socialism by East Europeans liberating themselves from the Soviet yoke: "Our problem is not to convince the Eastern Europeans that they can change regimes by Fabian [socialist] methods...Our duty, rather, is to go to the heart of the matter and to the fortress of advanced capitalism,...In other words, our task is to spread the conviction that a radical change of society in all its aspects is on our own historical agenda."

In other words, damn the disasters our crusades have created in the East, full speed ahead with our plans to destroy the capitalist democracies of the West. The enemy is within. Or, as *Time* columnist and Democratic Socialists of America chair Barbara Ehrenreich put it: "As a responsible radical, I believe our first responsibility is toward the evil close to home, and stopping that. In any event, I'm more worried in the long run about the belligerence of George Bush than of Saddam Hussein" (*Tikkun*, January 1991).

We see this destructive Left active today in America's universities, striving to discredit the very culture that created American democracy, attempting to smear America's heritage as the imperialist, patriarchal, racist construct of "dead white European males." And we see it in the streets, mobilized to oppose America's own right of self-determination and self-defense in an ongoing, relentless assault on America's military and intelligence communities which it maliciously portrays as the tentacles of a sinister "national security state."

In sum, what the Left has become — now that its fantasy of a socialist future has been exploded all over the world — is this: a nihilistic force whose goal is to deconstruct and dismantle America as a democracy and as a nation.

Revolution is a form of total war. The radical Left sees itself — has always seen itself — as part of an international revolutionary army. The archenemy of this international army is today, as it has been for the last forty-five years, the United States. Thus, *The Nation*, which is the most respected organ of the radical Left, defined the terms of the current battle over the Persian Gulf, in a front page editorial called "Choose Peace" in these words:

> The choice in the Persian Gulf conflict has never been between sanctions and force. It is between peace and war, between life and death. The party of death, which prefers self-descriptions that cover its thirst for conquest with appeals to the great tradition of just wars and lesser evils, has since August 2

seen sanctions as a kind of ritualistic foreplay to the violent penetration of
an entire region of the globe. President Bush manipulated the various United
Nations sanctions votes as he sent Secretary of State Baker to bribe and buy
a favorable "use of force" resolution, putting a specious international gloss
on his deadly designs for war. (December 24, 1990)

America is the "party of death" — this is the moral calculus of the
radical Left; George Bush's America — not Saddam Hussein's Iraq — is
the power with the "deadly designs for war" — this is what radicals
mean when they preach about peace.[§] □

[§]The following is a political song composed by "Voices for Peace" activists at
Dartmouth during the Persian Gulf War, to be sung to the tune of "America
the Beautiful:"

> Oh Beautiful,
> For racist lies,
> For homeless screams of pain;
> For purple lesions apathy,
> And bombs and acid rain.
> Amerika, Amerika,
> God cast a curse on thee!
> And spill the blood of brotherhood,
> That keeps oppressing me.

Chapter Four

Alex Goes to War

(Peter Collier)

Avoiding a reckoning is a habit of mind that not only characterizes Leftism as an intellectual pathology, but also the individuals who spread the disease. By not holding themselves accountable for what they say, let alone what the Left does, they allow themselves a profligacy of opinion and a no-fault analysis, emitting noxious ideas like gas and never acknowledging later on what a smell they have made.

There was enough gaseous rhetoric from the Left during the Gulf War, for instance, to reinflate the Hindenberg. Spokesmen and women outdid themselves in apocalyptic prediction and dire warning. How well did they do at handicapping History? For a thumbnail evaluation we need only look at the tout sheet of Alexander Cockburn, the contemporary Left's indispensable man.

Robespierre in residence at *The Nation* magazine and sometime columnist for *The Los Angeles Times, The Wall Street Journal*, and other papers in search of dishy extremism for their op-ed pages, Cockburn arrived on these shores in the Seventies. He is the most visible member of the Anglo-Irish clan that has come to function as something like the Jukes family of international Leftism. He has been delivering vatic opinions on the sickness and evil of American society for over a decade now, attracting a cult following at the frozen edges of the lunatic fringe. During that febrile moment of radical revival in the era of the nuclear "freeze" and the Sandinista takeover, Alex seemed to be on the crest of the wave. But the wave petered out. With the death of Leonid Brezhnev — Cockburn's last, best hope — a certain optimism went out of his work and he regretfully snuggled into the Luciferian *non serviam*. With

---

This artice appeared in the Second Thoughts Newsletter, *Spring 1991.*

the end of the Cold War, Alex had become the last of his breed, like those ragged Japanese soldiers who wandered the jungles of Asia for years, unaware that their side had lost.

George Will has called him the Last Stalinist, and suggests that the Smithsonian exhibit him behind glass. Yet Cockburn does have a certain appeal. He is a good read; he delivers up his execrable opinions with existential brio and a rabid unpredictability that make him capable of biting the hands that feed him. And unlike his Leftist comrades in the press, who now more than ever try to cloak their opinions in what they regard as liberal respectability, Cockburn says exactly what he thinks, no matter how daft or bloody-minded it may seem. He rags on the practitioners of *glasnost* for selling out the grand old cause. He engages in prolonged numerological debate not only with American Soviet experts but with Soviet experts on such issues as how many people were murdered by Joseph Stalin. (They say the figure is 30-50 million; Cockburn labors like a rat in heat to prove that only a tiny fraction of this number was killed, and, if pressed, he would probably say that they deserved it.) He affects an effortlessness, but obviously works hard at his craft, using a research assistant to comb arcane documents for facts which he then blends with his own malicious paranoia and serves up in essays that have the morbid fascination of Rorschach blots.

Always entertaining, if never right, Cockburn outdid himself in his writing about the Gulf War. The pieces he published during this time establish a record for flatulent wrong-headedness and radical wishful thinking, but because they epitomize the thinking of the Left, they are worth a replay. Alex got into the subject of the Gulf early. On September 24, 1990, he hurried to set up another credibility gap in his monthly column for *The Nation*. "Most Americans are temperamentally disposed to believe Big Oil is behind the whole thing," he said, "giving the nod to Saddam to take over Kuwait and thus, without much delay, double oil prices." Proceeding from a species of reasoning which used to be called vulgar Marxism but which, after the events of 1989, is now just vulgar, Cockburn goes on to advise the Iraqi public relations managers to stick to this theme in their efforts to affect U.S. policy because they could thereby "endear themselves to blue collar America." Although disgusted by the elephantine U.S. war machine lumbering toward the Gulf, Alex was nonetheless heartened by the belief that if it came to a showdown with Saddam, the American monster would probably break: "Knowledgeable fellows tell me that the M-1 tank was never tested in nose to nose deployment through sand; high speed fighter planes are of little use against tanks, as are the hand guided TOW and tank missiles in close engagements. The Stealth and B-52s are wildly inaccurate..."

Alex went on muttering about the buildup last fall. He continued spinning conspiracy theories in which the crisis was caused by Bush's plot, not Saddam's invasion. On December 24, he was able to parlay the countdown in the Gulf with another favorite hobby horse — the sell-out of Soviet reformers (Alex supports the KGB hardliners) — in a column charging that just-resigned Soviet Foreign Minister Shevardnadze was a "patsy" for the U.S. This was especially true on the issue of Kuwait, where Secretary of State Baker "was able to stampede, cajole and bribe the U.N. Security Council into a resolution sanctioning the use of force only because Shevardnadze signaled his support at a critical moment."

On January 17, the day after the beginning of the air war, Cockburn submitted his last column to *The Wall Street Journal*, that paper having decided to end his ten-year stint as a toy pit bull allowed to bite the op-ed page every couple of weeks. Seeing his departure as part of a *fin de siecle* event descending on the nation, Cockburn also delivered what would become the Left's party line on the war just begun: "The fighting and killing and dying on the Western side will be done to a disproportionate degree by people pressed into the military by economic hardship, using weapons badly made by manufacturers colluding with the Defense Department in the padded invoice and the faked test."

Two weeks later,, unable to deny any longer the efficacy of U.S. weapons, Cockburn, writing in *The Los Angeles Times* (February 3), set off a smoke screen. Having unearthed an obscure request by the Royal Air Force in 1919 to use mustard gas on Arabs during the British division of the spoils of the Ottoman Empire, a request Winston Churchill turned down, Cockburn suggested that that sort of casual genocide was taking place in Iraq. (Thus also setting up a moral equation whereby if Saddam used chemicals it could only be a delayed retaliation for something that didn't happen seventy-two years earlier.) Cockburn then upped the ante by predicting darkly that "today's applause" for the coalition bombing could be an "overture to tomorrow's calls for understanding if it becomes necessary to use nuclear weapons to overwhelm Iraq's intransigence." Adding a fillip of moral equivalence, he compared Bush and Saddam: "In moral texture there is little to separate the U.S. President from his Iraqi opposite number. The difference lies in their resources of violence." In this assertion, Alex proved himself a chip off the old block, his father, the Communist journalist Claud Cockburn, having tried to prove the moral equivalence of British leaders and the Nazis on the eve of World War II.

In his *Nation* column two weeks later, Alex said he had recently spoken to his brother Patrick, who was reporting from Baghdad for the English paper *The Independent*. Patrick had assured him that the bombing was having an effect quite opposite from the one intended. Before the air war, Iranian public opinion was against Saddam's invasion of Kuwait, but the bombing had "stiffened the will to resist" just as it did in Britain during the Blitz and in Vietnam. The mention of Britain encouraged Alex to cast a churlish eye at his old homeland and discover too many British military men who were "overweening and sarcastic about the fiber of the Iraqi fighting man." As an example of this hubris, he quoted derisively the officer who predicted that if a ground war came, "the major problem (of the coalition) would be accepting the surrender of thousands of Iraqi prisoners."

On March 4, in an article written for *The Nation* before the ground war began but published after it was over (because of the swift efficiency of the U.S. military whose equipment and morale he had spent the previous months deriding), Cockburn allowed himself to dream the impossible dream:

> Kuwait will most likely be vigorously contested, house by house, and just as the battle there could bog down, so too could the U.S. rush toward the rivers northwest of Basra come to grief. The very moment U.S. troops cross the border, tensions in the Arab and Islamic world, particularly in Iran, will multiply. Iraqis will be fighting on their nation's soil, which itself will be unforging as the troops enter difficult and marshy terrain near the ruins where the British Army met defeat at Kut in 1916....It is assumed in all Western countries that the U.S. and its allies must prevail. But it is not so long since 100,000 Iranian troops got within eyeshot of Basra, never reached that objective, and lost half their number. Is there any reason to suppose

that the West's victory is inevitable? In fact, the Iraqi triumph is conceivable, with the U.S. advance halted, the attack on Kuwait stalled, the casualties and reverses mounting at a rate beyond the power of military censors to suppress.

This ranks up there with the *Literary Digest* prediction that Alf Landon would defeat FDR. It would be nice to think that in some future column Alex might give us a *mea culpa* in which he admitted how wrong he was about everything — the inefficacy of U.S. weapons; the invigorating effect of U.S. bombing on Iraqi opinion; the superb fighting trim of the Iraqi military; the likelihood of a quagmire; the moral equivalence of Bush and Saddam; the significant possibility of a coalition defeat in the ground war. But such a reckoning runs against the grain of the Left. Don't look back; hustle on to the next crisis and start stacking the same old merchandise on the racks; that's Cockburn's interpretation, the Left's interpretation, of what journalism is all about.

As Truman Capote might have said, this is typing, not writing. But Alexander Cockburn is that history we often hear about that never learns and is therefore condemned to repeat itself. ◻

The War They Lost

(Peter Collier)

After several hours of CNN the first night of Desert Storm, I left my hotel room and went outside for some air. The quiet in San Francisco's Union Square was eerie: an air raid sort of stillness. Then came the echoes of approaching sounds bouncing off deserted streets. Suddenly a flying squad of people dressed in street action chic — a piece of pandemonium that had broken off a larger demonstration on Market Street — came into view. Shouting about oil companies, Iraq, George Bush and Vietnam, they paused for a moment to smash a storefront display window. As the shards of glass were collapsing onto the sidewalk in a slow motion fall, one of them, a man close to my own middle age, looked over and waved a casual clenched fist. "We're back in business now," he yelled, and then disappeared around a corner with the others.

It was a strange thing to say. Even stranger, I suppose, was the fact that I knew exactly what he meant. The business he was talking about was the business of the Sixties — that business of protest and rebellion, of breaking and entering the normal rhythms of daily life, of deconstructing America. This was the business he saw the Gulf War as starting up again. People were back in the street trashing things. The sword of dissidence was being pulled out of the stone of reaction. We were going back to the future of another Vietnam.

On the next day, day two of the air war, the demonstrations in San Francisco were massive, uncivil and disobedient. Some of the signs I saw bobbing in the crowds were protest postmodern: *Smell the New World Odor!* Others were decadent expressions of that old Sixties notion that the personal is political: *I'm Pissed Off!* But most of them proved

---

This article was a Second Thoughts Paper, *March 1991.*

that Vietnam was still the mother of all metaphors. *No More Vietnams!*
Another Vietnam in the Gulf! Even: *Hot Damn, Vietnam!*

The stakes were clear from the onset. This would be parallax war in
which the fighting might be done in Kuwait and Iraq but the ground to
be contested was Vietnam. Bush knew it: he had said that he wanted to
cut off the Vietnam experience and kill it. The Left was equally determined to protect Vietnam as its holy ground, the once and future war
in which America would be repeatedly humiliated. For the Left, it was
a meal ticket and ace-in-the-hole, the double bind in which it had
whiplashed this country for twenty years. *No More Vietnams* was the
sanction that kept this country impotent and unsure, and made sure
that it did not act in its own interests. *Another Vietnam* was what would
happen if it did manage to act, the debacle whose home truths the Left
would bring to the streets of America. *No More Vietnams* and *Another
Vietnam*: the warning and the wish; the liberals' fear and the radicals'
hope; the last refuge of the Left.

Listening to the speakers at these early anti-war rallies trying to find
that perfect pitch of outrage and vaunt that had worked so well in the
Sixties, I was struck by how often Vietnam was mentioned. It was the
inspirational message used for psyching up for the big game in the locker
room. It was like *Shazam!*, a word that transformed one thing
(Nicaragua, El Salvador, Iraq) into something else (Vietnam). As I
thought back, I remembered that twenty-five years ago, even when it
was still a war, Vietnam was also a metaphor. It was the heavy bulk on
the other side of every moral ledger; it was justification for every violent
thought or deed. When we hit cops with rocks back in the Sixties, what
they suffered was nothing compared to the agony of the Vietnamese
peasant. When we set fires in the universities it was nothing compared
to the napalming of a Vietnamese village. *Vietnam*: the word indicted
America and absolved those at home and abroad who took up arms
against it. It changed our political landscape. Before Vietnam the Left
had to be pro-Soviet; after Vietnam it was necessary only that it be
anti-American.

We experienced Vietnam as a cerebral tyranny in our lives long
before we admitted — those of us who finally did — that it was also a
tyrannical government. Yet even though we suspected that it was

morally stultifying, we allowed the war to acquire a hold over us because it also made things interesting, reshuffling the deck we were playing with and putting everything up for grabs. Vietnam had punched a hole in the cultural ozone, admitting revisionisms that made the U.S. responsible for everything leading up to and out of the Cold War and creating new time-space continua on which events like Wounded Knee and My Lai were welded into a single murderous reflex. Vietnam was religion. It conferred authenticity on believers in an addictive rush by giving them a feeling of separateness from and superiority to their own country, a country whose freedoms were a fraud and whose democracy was a sham. That sense of being a resident alien, of having escaped the malign gravity of patriotism: this was the drug of Vietnam. No wonder that for many radicals the greatest fear was that some day the war might end.

For some of the people in the early demonstrations against Desert Storm — still addicts of Vietnam — it never had ended. There had just been a long cease fire. For them, Vietnam had all the authority of history, but none of the moral complexity. It was history frozen in the scenes of people desperately clinging to the skids of helicopters trying to lift off from the Saigon embassy; history with only a beginning and middle, but not the end of 1975 and beyond, all those year zeros of political reeducation camps, boat people, and genocide. For a generation the Left had had its cake and eaten it — talking of Vietnam as if it were history while using it as a political blunt instrument.

No More Vietnams/ Another Vietnam had worked so long and so well that those protesting this new war were certain it would allow them to break the sorcery of the Reagan era. The night before the air war began, Left-wing Congresswoman Barbara Boxer exulted on San Francisco television that the anti-war movement was already far bigger than it had been several years into Vietnam: "And the war has not even started yet!" Just think what would happen when the firing began! Once the template of Vietnam could be laid over events in the Gulf everything else was guaranteed. The law of General Giap would come into operation: the U.S., which could not be beaten on a foreign battlefield, would certainly be defeated on the streets of America.

In that first flush of excitement, the anti-war movement's hyperbole was as extreme as Saddam's. He talked about punishing the infidels; they talked about paralyzing America. He talked about U.S. soldiers wading through rivers of gore, drowning in their own blood, and returning home in dwarf coffins. The anti-war spokesmen talked about body bags, *tens of thousands* of them. They enumerated the body bags the way a miser counts his wealth. They were angry in advance that television news would be prohibited from showing the offloading of military corpses in the U.S. This would deprive them of proof that they were right.

* * *

Over the next few weeks many amazing things happened. The high-tech weapons Reagan had been criticized for building during his eight years of genial inattention worked to perfection. And so did the military whose morale, pay, and stature his administration had improved. It was a paradox. For the anti-war movement our loss in Vietnam had been a sweet victory; for the Army it had been a terrible defeat. Yet the military was one institution in American life that had walled itself off from defeatism with the same rigor that it had walled itself off from AIDS. It had kept alive its sense of mission and honor. It only asked Rambo's much maligned question: "Do we get to win this time?" And when answered in the affirmative, the military said it was good to go.

It was also amazing to watch the media. Television went to the Mideast looking for the kind of television war it created in Vietnam and got a television war of quite another kind. The military rules which forced the media to report events rather than shape them caused the convening of many roundtable discussions back home and discomfort that was almost hemorrhoidal on the part of Bill Moyers and other Leftists in liberals' clothing. The media kept looking for Tet in all the wrong places — in the suicide attack by Iraqi armor on Khafji; in those first deaths by friendly fire. Then, when Tet came in the hundred-hour land war that routed the Iraqi Army, the media had no alternative but to report it as a victory instead of a defeat.

Most amazing of all, however, was the utter inconsequence of this anti-war movement. Armed to the teeth with the hopes and fears of another Vietnam, a fortification that seemed impregnable and a firepower that seemed invincible, it put up even less of a struggle than the Republican Guard.

What happened? Why didn't it come out to fight? Anti-war leaders would complain, in what passes for self examination on the Left, that the war was just too short; that it was too antiseptic; that the television reports were slanted against them; and, of course, that there had not been enough body bags. "How can you have an anti-war movement without a war?" the late Abbie Hoffman had asked mournfully a few years ago during the days when he and other refugees from Vietnam were waiting impatiently for something to happen in Central America. If he were alive today, he probably would have asked with that same melancholy sense of betrayal, "How can you have an anti-war movement without body bags?"

The real problem for the Left was that it relied on the power of a word — *Vietnam* — to carry the day. Simply saying the word over and over in an incantatory way was supposed to make the thing happen. They were so certain of the power of the Vietnam metaphor, so heavily invested in the similarities between then and now that they ignored the differences. They were so busy with their Marxist cant about international oil companies that they forgot Marx's quaint warning about history appearing first as tragedy and then repeating itself later on as farce.

Caught up in its nightclub imitation of moral witness, the Left forgot all that had been required to make the first Vietnam happen. First and foremost was the need to romanticize the enemy. Saddam presented a problem. It would be a little hard to make him the George Washington of his people, as we had Uncle Ho twenty-five years ago. He did not exactly hide behind Zen mystery, and so it would be impossible to ignore his evil, such as the gassing of the Kurds, as we had ignored Ho's slaughter of his dissidents and Trotskyites twenty-five years ago.

There was also the problem of Iraqi society itself. The Left might develop tedious arguments to defend Kuwait's status as the 19th province, and natter on about how the British, our kissing cousins in imperialism, had created the corrupt boundaries of the Gulf states in the first place. But it was impossible to romanticize the Iraqis, as we had the Vietnamese. There would be no Frances Fitzgerald writing a Mideast *Fire in the Lake* about the soulful poetry and tensile strengths of the Iraqi world-view. Revolutionary pilgrims (except for the egregious Louis Farrakhan) would not travel to Baghdad and return, as Tom Hayden and others did in the Sixties, to say that they had been over into a future that not only worked but was more moral than the present, a future comprised of a "gentle Confucian Communism" such as the world had not yet seen.

Because it could not ennoble the Iraqis or their leaders, in other words, the Left was denied access to that fraudulent equation that had worked with such clockwork precision in the case of Vietnam — the equation which held that since the enemy were blameless peasants seeking only to build a little corner of utopia, then the U.S., which was trying to destroy them, must necessarily be a hell on earth to be combatted (in one of the odious little catch phrases of the Sixties) by any means necessary.

The Left's final miscalculation in the matter of the Gulf War involved the American people. Scornful of them as always, seeing them as debased and manipulated, believing that love of country can only be *kitsch*, the anti-war movement assumed that they would be demoralized by its juggernaut, as they had been in the Sixties. But they, the anonymous people of the middle ground, understood this war from the beginning. They knew what the stakes were. They knew as well as the Left did that what was happening in the Gulf was not about Kuwait or Iraq but about America — whether this country could open fire without shooting itself in the foot; whether it was a good and generous country or the evil empire of the Left's fantasies.

This 85% may not have known who General Giap was but they remembered how the U.S. *was* defeated on the streets of America twenty years ago and were determined to get out there themselves this time. They seized the initiative and defined the issues so that the Left was deprived of one of the assets that had been so important the last time — hating the troops, stigmatizing them as baby killers and genocidal mercenaries in the service of Amerika. The people who supported this war were so strong that they forced the protesters into a grudging popular frontism of supporting the military if not the mission, a disingenuous me-toosim that obviously grated on those forced to practice it and evaporated long before it was time to welcome the troops home.

In the end the anti-war movement turned out to be not a movement at all, but a confederation of narcissisms ranging from ACTUPers to animal rightists; a collection of grievances about America unloosed twenty-five years ago and now grown so unruly that they were unable to subordinate their single issues to a larger purpose. Rather than being the nucleus of something new, this movement turned out to be the residue of something old. In trying to manufacture another Vietnam, the anti-war protesters managed only to produce a nostalgic pageant in which they resembled nothing quite so much as those people who dress up in Civil War uniforms every summer and reenact the Battle of Gettysburg.

* * *

Since the war's end, commentators have talked about who the losers were. Saddam, King Hussein, and the PLO always head the list. Yet the losing leaders and organizations lost only land, prestige, weapons, armies. The real loser is the American Left. It lost everything.

When the Cold War ended the Left could deny, in one of those sudden episodes of moral amnesia to which it is prone, that it was never invested in the other side and claim that at any rate that this had been a Soviet loss, not an American victory. The Gulf War left no such wiggle room. Here the Left not only lost the war, but it lost Vietnam as well, its Camelot and its Holy Grail. Now Vietnam is once again what it actually always was — the aberration, not the norm; just another war.

The Left will now retreat to the governments in exile it has established in the universities of America and begin to wage the long war over the meaning of the war. It will also continue to enforce the smelly little orthodoxies of political correctness. But something has gone out of the enterprise; it has developed a slow leak. The only thing that will save the Left is some future U.S. disaster that will give it back its homeland in another Vietnam. □

Second Thoughts:
Former Radicals Look Back at the Sixties

Edited by Peter Collier and David Horowitz

Twenty former radicals of the Sixties recount their political journeys — how they became disillusioned with the New Left, how they extricated themselves from their radical ties, and how they finally came out of the political closet. Black activist Julius Lester describes his moment of truth during a Black Panther trial, author and film critic Michael Medved reports on the radical chic in Hollywood that makes "airhead activists" out of brat pack stars and starlets; Robert Leiken tells of the McCarthyite attacks he suffered at the hands of the Left as a reprisal for his criticisms of the Sandinistas; and on the lighter side, former *National Lampoon* editor P.J. O'Rourke divulges that his second thoughts began when a Leftist gang stole his girlfriend. Among the other contributors are Joshua Muravchik, Rev. Richard Neuhaus, Michael Novak, David Ifshin, Scott McConnell, Glenn Loury, Arturo Cruz, Jr., Jeffrey Herf, K.L. Billingsley, Doan Van Toai, Ronald Radosh, and Barry Rubin. This significant document gives rare insight into the intersection between the personal and the political. It captures a unique moment when members of a radical generation talk about finally coming home again.

288 pages — $12.95, Softcover

Peter Collier and David Horowitz are best-selling authors of
The Rockefellers, The Kennedys, The Fords, and *Destructive Generation.*

Second Thoughts About Race in America

Edited by Peter Collier and David Horowitz

What happened to civil rights? How did the concept of equal opportunity get mugged by the ideology of equality of outcome? Why did the emphasis in the struggle for racial justice shift from the individual to the group? How did matters of race get mixed up with the orthodoxies of "political correctness?"

To answer these and other questions, best-selling authors Peter Collier and David Horowitz reconvened late last year some of the "second thoughters," whose first conference was chronicled in their recent book *Second Thoughts: Former Radicals Look Back at the Sixties.* In this new meeting veterans of the Movement use their experiences from the Sixties as a fulcrum to discuss the growing tension between the new civil rights standard and the old.

The contributors include former Chairman of the U.S. Commission on Civil Rights, William B. Allen; Shelby Steele, author of *The Content of Our Character*; *Washington Post* reporter Juan Williams, author of *Eyes on the Prize*; syndicated columnist Richard Cohen; Stanley Crouch, former staff writer at *The Village Voice* and author of *Notes of a Hanging Judge*; Brooklyn Law School professor Henry Mark Holzer, author of *Sweet Land of Liberty*; political correspondent Joe Klein, author of *Payback: Five Marines After Vietnam*; former SNCC organizer and University of Massachusetts Judaic Studies professor Julius Lester; Harvard University political economist Glenn Loury, author of *Free at Last? Racial Advocacy in the Post-Civil Rights Era*; C.U.N.Y. History professor Ronald Radosh; former Editor-in-Chief of the *Dartmouth Review* Harmeet Singh Dhillon; Abigail Thernstrom, author of *Whose Votes Count*; writer Frederick Robinson; and syndicated columnist and George Mason University economist Walter Williams, author of *All It Takes Is Guts*.

175 pages — $17.95, Hardcover